SACHEVERELL SITWELL

A Symposium

Portrait of Sacheverell Sitwell by Cecil Beaton

SACHEVERELL
SITWELL

A Symposium

EDITED BY
DEREK PARKER

BERTRAM ROTA

Contents

Prefatory Note

The contributors to this tribute were without exception delighted to make their contributions; this does not mean that they should not be thanked for doing so. It should also be said that some of them wished to make their tributes longer, but for various reasons were unable to do so.

John Smith's essay on Sacheverell Sitwell's poetry first appeared in *Poetry Review*, and Denys Sutton's essay on his appreciation of the visual arts, in *Apollo*; both have been to some extent amended and re-written.

The frontispiece photograph of Sir Sacheverell Sitwell is by Sir Cecil Beaton; that facing p. 50 by Christopher Angeloglou; the latter is reproduced by permission of *The Sunday Times*.

The original idea for this book was that of Geoffrey Elborn, for whose assistance in its preparation I am also grateful.

D.P.

Introduction

Sitting in the drawing-room at Weston, while the poet's wife embroidered a mitre for an adjacent bishop, we had listened to Scarlatti, talked of Liszt, Tiepolo, Modigliani, Torcello; and, at ten-thirty, the poet wheeled a television set from a far corner of the room, and said: 'And now perhaps you would not object to watching a little all-in wrestling?' And we watched, with considerable pleasure, the lightning brown Masambula giving Mr. Brian 'Gold Belt' Maxime a well-deserved come-uppance.

I remembered that scene some years later, when listening to Sir Sacheverell Sitwell choosing the music with which he would hope to be stranded on Roy Plomley's desert island—not, as one might have thought, a toccata of Galuppi, or a madrigal of Monteverdi, but a scene from *Carmen*, and a rollicking finale, *Ogni cura si dona al diletto*, from Verdi's *Un Ballo in Maschera*. The point being that Sir Sacheverell, far from being an exquisite interested only in a rapt contemplation of the 'precious', is and I would guess always has been also very much in touch with the kind of art which means most to the average, educated Englishman. This is not to say that he has not, often, been ahead of his time—certainly this was so between the wars, when he played a part in educating the taste of that time—but that he has had an instinct for the *general*, as well as a knowledge of the particular.

This has been misunderstood by a number of critics, often I suspect because they associated him with his brother and sister, whose instincts in art were, I fancy, rather different. They were, as Dame Edith put it, always 'a little outside life'; her younger brother has never been that, except in the sense that all poets are. This has dismayed the critics, as critics always are dismayed by writers they cannot easily categorise; and since Sir Sacheverell is a writer who has preferred to use and develop his own voice, and has not bowed to changing styles and attitudes, they have too often preferred others who (as Jane Austen put it) were 'of strong, natural, sterling insignificance, though adorned in the first style of fashion'. I think that it cannot be denied, either, that all three Sitwells suffered somewhat because of their membership of a family of considerable age and nobility; once rather an advantage for a writer, this was certainly no help in the twentieth century, except in obtaining for them the wrong sort of publicity and possibly even in the first instance the wrong sort of audience.

However that may be, nothing prepared me for the shock of reading, in my teens, the overwhelming poem *Agamemnon's Tomb*, in *Canons of Giant Art* (1933), which said and still says everything I too feel about death:

You are dead, you are dead, and all the dead are nothing to us,
There's nothing, nothing, nothing, not a breath beyond:
O give up every hope of it, we'll wake no more,
We are the world and it will end with us:
The heart is not a clock, it will not wind again,
The dead are but dead, there is no use for them,
They neither care, nor care not, they are only dead.

It was that note which drew me first to Sacheverell Sitwell's work: it shows a vein in his character—a deep inbred, civilised pessimism—which contributed a great deal to his understanding of the strange character of Liszt, and gave him a special insight into the profundity beneath the glittering surface of Scarlatti's greatest sonatas. And if I am not mistaken, it also informs his writing on architecture, and gives additional poignancy

to his descriptions of lesser forms of art. It is a vein in
which a chill still runs: over thirty years later, in a poem
written not long after the death of his sister, he was to
write:

> His blood colours my cheek.
> Ah! but when that blood is no longer there;
> I saw that, I saw that.
> When the live thing had just gone,
>   Was those few seconds gone,
> Gone where,
>   where, where?

It may be that this profound pessimism has been one
of the reasons why Sir Sacheverell has written so much:
'melancholy', Dr. Johnson said, 'should be diverted by
every means but drinking.' And melancholy does not
mean, of course—as a great number of writers has
demonstrated—that we must always be serious, much
less solemn. The enormous vivacity and variety of the
poet's books dazzles: a man who can write as wonderfully
of the splendours and miseries of the world, and in almost
the same paragraph can turn to elegant gossip, an essay
on Robbie Ross or Margot Fonteyn, an Introduction to a
catalogue of historic wallpaper designs or a book of
fashion plates, a book on German Baroque sculpture or
the topography of Malta—such a man, in an age of more
or less dull specialisation, deserves to be celebrated as
he is celebrated in this book, by his friends and admirers.
Sacheverell Sitwell, like any creative artist, must from
time to time wonder what, among his work, will survive
or not survive. It is a fruitless occupation: the true value
of a contemporary book is in what it means to its contemporaries, and his books have spoken to us of emotions,
people, societies, works of art, which we all thought we
knew, but which we have rediscovered through his pages.
'A book', Thoreau argued, 'should contain pure discoveries, glimpses of terra firma, though by shipwrecked

mariners, and not the art of navigation by those who have never been out of sight of land.' Sir Sacheverell has steered himself across most known seas, and many unfamiliar ones, in his encyclopaedic travels in the worlds of the eye and the ear and the mind. His shipwrecks have been on those rocks we all know; his maps have enriched our knowledge of how to meet them, of their sharpness, of how to sight and avoid them, or how to ensure that they do not utterly destroy us. Saluting him, we commend him to fellow-voyagers.

D.P.

Never a Dull Moment
Georgia Sitwell

I was introduced to Osbert Sitwell at a dance given by Arnold Bennett, whom we had met staying with the Beaverbrooks in the country.

I had heard a lot about the three Sitwells and longed to meet them; I was very, very high-brow in those days, quite different to what I am now. I tend to get lower and lower-brow (Cyril Connolly invented that splendid term 'near-brow' and I have sunk to that). Anyway, I went to tea at Carlyle Square and there was Sachie.

We had tea in the dining room, which was a converted garden-shed, very attractively decorated to give it a subterranean feeling with the famous marine furniture, and after a little while he leaned across the table and said 'Have another saandwich.' I remember so well it was the first time I heard his curious pronunciation of 'a's'.

I had read *Southern Baroque Art, One Hundred and One Harlequins*, etc., and I marvelled. His personality and appearance were not disappointing and I ate several more sandwiches. Then he strolled upstairs after me to the drawing room and said 'Will you come and dine with me one night?'

I said 'Of course I'd love to.'

In those days, well brought up young ladies were not supposed to have dinner alone with a man and I was still only 18, but fortunately fairly spirited and my father was away. So I said to my mother 'I am going out with Sachie Sitwell' and I went. He took me to 'Stop Flirting' and we had supper afterwards at the Savoy Grill and have never really looked back since. We married 18 months later. It took me that long to make up my mind, as I feared I had bitten off more than I could chew.

It was a formidable family to become a part of, but Edith was always perfectly marvellous—so sweet and warm and interested. She really adored Sachie and one of the first things she ever said to me was 'I know I am going to love you because you love Sachie.'

From the beginning it was of course fascinating for me to be in Sachie's company—I always wanted to learn and realised how little I knew, although I may say I was far better educated than most English girls of my age. For instance, at the first school I went to in Montreal, one began at the age of 9 to read Greek mythology, then Chinese legends and then Roman history. We met the head girl of 'Miss Edgar's and Miss Cramp's' in Venice and she said 'Do you know, after I left school I couldn't speak to a man because I knew too much.'

The system was to begin with Ancient History and then proceed until one got to the stage of studying maps of the War (1914–18).

Travelling with Sachie has been the most wonderful experience; there have certainly been a lot of nervous moments, but life has not been dull. You can't imagine how agitated and agitating it is to travel with him because he is so highly strung, nervous and apprehensive, though as both Osbert and Sachie had been in the Army, they had been trained to be punctual and conventional in many ways and in all the years I have managed only once to miss a train and he never has.

He has a remarkably photographic mind; never makes notes, or hardly ever. He writes down what he has seen and liked most in a picture gallery, but not at the time, and for years afterwards he is able to remember not only what he has seen, but the people with whom he saw it.

Of course it is wonderful for the person who accompanies him, because now I never have to look at a guide book, hardly ever at a book of reference, I just ask questions, although it often irritates him!

I think the countries he has enjoyed most are Japan

and Mexico and Cambodia. He adored Japan—a new kind of people, a different point of view and a new music. Music, perhaps, is his main interest, music of all kinds. I often tell him that he likes too much music, that he is not selective enough. And it can't be too loud for him. The minute I have left the room (I usually go to bed just before he does) he turns it on louder.

He enjoys simple pleasures, teasing me, listening to musical comedy scores and complaining about pop art. He is the most versatile and gregarious person imaginable. He doesn't like talking about his own work and is just as happy gossiping to my women friends as he is, except with very few people, discussing his work or more serious subjects.

He is a compulsive worker, sitting at his desk in the morning from 9.30 to at least 12.30 and then again from 5 to 7 regularly. He never stops working because he is not in the mood, he treats it like an office job.

But he is a countryman at heart, loves the dogs and adores country landscape, although he is not the sort of person who would go out, as I always used to think poets did, when it was raining and say 'My God, the beauty of this landscape!' He will say 'I am going to catch cold, I must get my mackintosh.' But at the same time, beauty of nature means a lot to him.

He is first and foremost a poet, although a number of his books, the travel books for instance, have been written to try and make money in order to provide the creature comforts which we both appreciate so much and indeed depend on. We are both martyrs to comfort and love good food, so in a way I suppose we are not the children of our age at all. Nobody has ever been better company.

Our elder son's coloured nanny used to say 'We haven't got much money, but we do see life!'

Never a dull moment and with poetry never far from the surface.

Foi d'Esthète · *Cyril Connolly*

I first met all the Sitwells in one swoop when they descended on the Washington Irving Hotel in Granada at Easter 1925. I was then an undergraduate, exploring Spain for myself, and I found the friendship which they extended to me on my lonely evenings quite intoxicating. They and their companions Willie Walton and Richard Wyndham all wore black cloaks and Andalusian hats. At first I wasn't sure it could be them until they began to express an animated concern about the high cost of living in Scarborough, one of their solemn jokes to discourage advances from the other guests, mostly military couples from Gibraltar. Edith talked to me about poetry. I was a great admirer of her *Sleeping Beauty*, and when I told her that some of us at Oxford had a passion for *The Waste Land* she remarked: 'I will tell Tom when we get back. He *will* be delighted.'

Osbert liked anecdotes and Sachie, I remember, had an inexhaustible curiosity about places. 'You've been to Huercal Overa—now what's *that* like?' I have described this meeting before, since I can't seem to start any account of the Sitwells without it. They combined art with dandyism, the only valid alternative to Bloomsbury. However, I was too shy to accept Edith's first invitation, and it was Dick Wyndham who became my life-long friend, the Sitwells only swimming back into my orbit with the war years.

'Sachie' now became 'Sachie and Georgia', one of the most permanently devoted couples it is possible to imagine, a beacon to all their friends for the best part of a life-time. One had only to encounter them for a moment to see how inevitably right it was that the sensitive poet with his omnivorous antennae for all that was strange or marvellous in the visual arts should depend on the glowing dark beauty of this practical and life-enhancing Canadian (sister of the actress Frances Doble) for the devotion and constant companionship necessary to carry him through his aesthetic adventures.

For the Sitwells were not really happy people. Through Arthur Waley, who had such an admiration for Sachie's early poetry, I caught many a glimpse of him. Like his brother and, to a much greater extent, his sister, he was particularly sensitive to snubs and rebuffs and the endless abrasions from the Philistines—and this I think because all three had a particular awareness of the sadness and transitoriness of things, a homesickness for Eden found in Edith's poetry, in their *Colonel Fantock* fantasies, in Sacheverell's autobiography *All Summer In a Day* . . . Apprehension of beauty, awareness of loss: even the remotest epochs are marinated by his poetic imagination. I open a page at random:

We do not see him, yet. But in another moment, he stands at bay in a little clearing and we behold this ghost from the age of giants. His stature is a matter for astonishment even if you are prepared for it. And so rare has he become that his every appearance cannot fail to strike with this effect. Like all ghosts the giant elk is colourless. That is to say, he is black or gray. In certain lights he is the white elk, as at this moment in an autumn morning. So immense is the span of his antlers that they must have had some other purpose than ornament or self-defence. It could not have been for mere battle . . . Spears are couched, and the elk runs again and again upon them, bending the thin shafts. Some twenty or thirty hounds together pull him to the ground. The huntsmen put their bronze swords into him with a soft, heavy sound. His mouth and tongue drop blood and he raises, or attempts to raise his head, as though to try his crown. The dying of the giant elk is a piteous sight, and it should be a parable to the King who stands before him. In a moment his tower of fronds totters, then lifts again, and leans and falls.

In all the land there may not have been more than a hundred families of these gigantic deer.

And he goes on to describe the pair of horns in the tapestry room at Hardwick: 'in the grey silence of that paradise of needlework . . . it was the memory of them, in childhood, that determined me to write of this.' (*Primitive Scenes & Festivals.*)

And so back to that extraordinary childhood where the two brothers and their sister, owing to their father's monolithic egotism, really grew up as three only children.

But it must not be thought that this poetic nostalgia held him back from exploration of the present world; it rather stimulated his curiosity to see everything that he could before finding his way back. As he says of himself there is hardly a remarkable building or statue or landscape or city or work of art that he has not seen or musical composition that he has not heard. Osbert's remark that anyone who could visit Angkor and didn't was mad does not apply to him for he has written one of the best books about it. Mexico, Spain, Italy, Holland, Morocco, Portugal are all subjects of his quest and his *Southern Baroque Art* in 1924 was a milestone in the development of our modern sensibility. 'A study of painting, architecture and music in Italy and Spain of the 17th and 18th centuries' is the subtitle. It put Lecce on the aesthetic map, as his brother was to put Noto, but also Caserta and Braga and he was soon to follow it up with books on the South German rococo its architecture and sculpture. His *British Architects and Craftsmen* (1945) was one of the books that preserved my sanity in the last war, though I seem to remember a tribute to Venice rather more clearly than anything else. ['I am Italian by training . . . my school was Venice. . . .']

When we first meet Sacheverell Sitwell, now a baronet, one can find the experience disconcerting, even intimidating. That is because his mind takes us round a kind of obstacle course, like a don giving us a general knowledge viva and determined to get one through. He relishes the misfortunes of great artists because they illustrate the crushing power of the Philistine. The hidden '*brutto poter*' of nature triumphs; painters go blind, composers deaf,

6

writers starve. 'Ah, Cyril—and how is your tax problem?' 'Terrible. The State is determined to ruin me.' 'So is mine. But at least you have enough to eat. Not like Modigliani.' 'And Darley I believe starved to death.' 'And so did Otway. Schönberg was absolutely destitute.' 'And how are your roses?' 'Did you know that Zephyrine Drouin was discovered growing wild in Turkey? They say the scent of roses will soon be quite extinct, like musk. By the way, myrrh and frankincense were both trees. And honeydew was excreted by an aphis. Have you read the new book about Coleridge? The man from Porlock is an invention. And you say you never knew Peter Warlock?' 'Yes, I did meet him once or twice.' 'He put the cat out before he killed himself.' 'What happened to it?' 'I think it went to Constant. And there was that great bibliophile and librarian who was so cold he had to cover himself with folios.' 'Better than burning them.' 'I don't know which was worse, the burning of Byron's journals by people who should have known better or Lady Burton burning her husband's great work on homosexuality because he told her to in a dream.' 'Dowson wrote a good poem about it.' 'Poor Dowson, he spilled—not a tidy man like Beardsley. And,' (with renewed solicitude) 'how are *you*?'

In his *British Architects and Craftsmen*, in which he writes so well about Gibbs and Ditchley, about Hardwick with 'the most beautiful room in Europe', about the fallen Venetian marbles of Sutton Scarsdale and the interior of 44, Berkeley Square, Kent's little-known masterpiece in London, before it became glorious as the Clermont Club, there is a gleam of autobiography. 'Particularly I admired, and still do, the Banquet of Anthony and Cleopatra at the Palazzo Labia. Never, never shall I forget, for it is my belief and faith, the only religion that I have ever had, the negro in green velvet holding a flask of wine. . . .' *Foi d'esthète*, which is just as profound and lasting as other faiths and also has its saints and martyrs who devote their sensibility to enriching ours while the stench of vulgarity, cruelty, mammon and cement mounts ever

higher. Fifty years of unrewarded and scarcely acknow-
ledged devotion since his visit to the South. 'Where I
made my name, for what little it was worth.'

Lately Sir Sacheverell has brought out thirteen slim
volumes of recent poetry, volumes dealing with many
botanical subjects, hyacinths, cacti, strawberries, auriculas
and even parrots. My favourite is the book on roses, and
here again is another autobiographical gleam if we know
that his maternal grandmother with the portcullis crest,
was a Somerset:

Red rose of the portcullis
　　from whom I have a drop of that rose-blood in my veins,
Or am at least brother to that pretendant,
　　Now fading, falling as we all must

I have not yet felt the drag or weight,
　　but for how much longer can that be,
Who have still your pollen
　　though I cannot pollinate?

Blackspot and rust are all around to see
　　the wrecks of two persons are all that now remains,
Whom I loved more than they loved me

But the beauty and poetry
　　I learned from her
Are antidotes to all self-pity.

The Desperate Romantic · *C. P. Snow*

The Sitwells used to be spoken of as though they were a collective entity, or effectively indistinguishable. The same thing happened to the Brontës. In both cases it was peculiarly absurd. Charlotte Brontë is about as different from Emily as two writers in the same language at the same period can reasonably be. In all essential matters, that applies to Sacheverell Sitwell in relation to his elder brother and—a shade less comprehensively—to his sister. His gifts, which are great, are different in kind from theirs. He has depths of imaginative intensity which Osbert neither could have reached nor probably, knowing his own talent, would have wished to. In that respect Sacheverell is the more unusual writer: and he paid a corresponding price in being less professional, to use an over-worked term, than the other two.

The three of them gained a great deal from their solidarity, and when, in the early twenties, they were taunting commonplace opinion, they were a major support to each other. But in all combinations of artistic people, there are bound to be some sacrifices to be made, and maybe some distortions of personality. Osbert, I should guess, though I met him only as a remote acquaintance, was the least affected. Dame Edith, whom I knew and loved, suffered in her own literary struggles and was also, because of her integral loyalty, vulnerable through any hostility to the other two. Sacheverell made a sacrifice in two ways. His own profound originality tended to be overlooked, and is still overlooked, as a consequence of being one of a combination. Further, his temperament, as well as his art, really was not made for collective literary warfare, or for literary warfare of any kind.

All three were sensitive quite beyond the ordinary. Like all other writers one can think of, they were wounded by criticism, particularly by the vindictively personal, almost physical, criticism which they aroused. They had the ill-luck to attract a specific kind of envy. Dame Edith sometimes used to attribute this to political enmity. I don't think that was true. It was more that their life-styles and attitudes, their air of amiable loftiness and superbity, evoked rancour in persons who had the desire to cut down the tall poppies. And the fact that the Sitwells were also excessively generous and magnanimous didn't protect them, but the reverse. The only reward artists get for generosity is in heaven. It is much wiser, in the snakes and ladders of literary reputation, to be mean-spirited.

Meeting this eruption of rancour, the three of them responded in different fashions, even when they presented a united front to the world. Osbert, and even more Dame Edith, fought back. Insult had to be repaid by insult. Dame Edith was hurt, she didn't in her heart like the activity, but she gained a certain amusement or exhilaration from it. Whereas Sacheverell did not like it at all. His own response, if he had been solitary, would have led him to relapse into silence. Let the mob scream. This response might not be as self-healing as the others' active one. You lose a bit of dignity by meeting claw with claw, but it is likely to be therapeutic. So, in many ways the strangest of the three, Sacheverell may have been the most affected, which has meant a loss for the rest of us, for he hasn't produced as much as once seemed likely. This is sad. Still, he has written books, quite unlike not only those of his brother and sister, but anything published in England in the last fifty years.

Some time ago Pamela Hansford Johnson wrote an article about him called *On Being the Wrong Size*. Her thesis was that he was too non-conformist, too ill-fitting, in various dimensions too large, to suit the scaling-down predilections of our time. I agreed with her when she wrote that, and do so still. His best work—*Splendours and Miseries, The Quick and The Dead, Journey to the Ends of Time*

10

(of which disappointingly only the first volume has appeared)—is startling in its power. A good many writers since the First World War have told us about the horrors of the human condition: but he is alone in his blend of cultivated civility and macabre imaginative insight.

No one has ever been more capable of producing a cold grue down the spine. This is only one of his literary effects, but it has to be stressed because it is the expression of a unique tension between one side of his artistic persona, excessively civilised, a man of taste in the eighteenth-century fashion, world traveller, connoisseur of the visual arts (he has a naturally acute eye, which has been most carefully trained), and the hidden side, more profound, deeply suspicious of all men's depravity and his own.

The danger, and the misreading, is to treat him as a classical artist, frigid, lightweight, and urbane. All three adjectives are contradictions of the truth. Under the surface of connoisseurship, he is wildly romantic in the most desperate fashion. His ultimate imagination is much more like Dickens at his darkest than Jane Austen. Even his visual taste, which is much more controlled than the best of his writing (this occurs when he allows the curbs of amenity to slip away), runs to the baroque. His sense of human experience has its own outward shape of the baroque, with wild and whirling decorations. Underneath that, there is the feeling for the romantic agony. Underneath that again his gaze is steady, and what he sees is jet-black.

Readers in the future are going to discover him with a shock, as something utterly unlike their conception of his kind of civilisation. The process might be hurried up, if someone at the present moment had the good sense to make a selection—in total, up to the length of a fair-sized novel—from his work. There aren't many writers who could be represented so dramatically by such a selection, or whose quality would beam more clearly through.

11

A Pilgrimage
to Beauty · *Raymond Mortimer*

A sister and two brothers, each of them tall and fair, talk and laugh with me in the formal Renishaw garden. The gaiety contrasts with the sadness of their once so beautiful mother, sitting in her tapestried drawing-room, and the severity of their courteous but formidable father, isolated at his own choice, and now safely out of earshot, gazing statuesque at his park, while he ponders further, more extravagant landscapings. Such is the picture I have prized for half a century.

That was a golden age, though darkened by unemployment: no enemy threatened war; all the arts brimmed with vitality; and to be young was very heaven. In France painting had reached a new summit, Paul Valéry had resumed his versification, Aragon and Eluard had started on theirs; Proust was still completing his prodigious novel, Mauriac and Paul Morand had revealed their extraordinary gifts, Cocteau was astonishing us with his versatility. In England Yeats and D. H. Lawrence, each near his apogee, Eliot, Virginia Woolf, Ronald Firbank and Arthur Waley, together with the three Sitwells, kept us continually on the delicious *qui vive*.

The precocious Sacheverell enchanted me from the first with his elegance and sweetness as well as with the high promise of his writings. We shared many interests. Like all my friends, he was a devotee of the Diaghilev Ballet and of current painting. Also I had written in 1921 an article in *The London Mercury* applauding the then utterly despised Baroque of Rome, and then hastened to Lecce; but his knowledge of the vigorous Baroque, and its delicate offspring, the Rococo, soon far outstripped mine.

What I have always valued most in him is the poetic

12

imagination. Although that makes radiant the whole of *All Summer in a Day*, and glitters in all his other prose, I happen to prefer poetry that is in verse (with rare exceptions, such as Jeremy Taylor and Bossuet, Chateaubriand and De Quincey). My favourite of all his books is *Canons of Giant Art*, a long poem finely maintained, at a time when most poets were at their best in the sprint. I fiercely regret that in the thirty-six intervening years he has given us hardly anything but prose.

Recently, however, I have had the luck to read thirteen slim, paper-bound volumes of his verse, produced as it were clandestinely, like the *samizdat* behind the Iron Curtain, although goodness knows our Director of Public Prosecutions could detect nothing in them that might corrupt us, or even our servants. The subjects are usually those he has always found inspiring—flowers, fruit, birds, landscapes, palaces, monasteries, paintings, carvings, *coloratura* singing, the *Commedia dell'Arte*, girls with magnolia skin and ships with masts turning into vines. All his five senses are superbly responsive.

The curiosity that keeps him so young has made him not only an insatiable reader but a traveller over five continents, seeking for whatever might fire his fancy from Cambodia to Guatemala. In Japan, for instance, he found landscapes that looked as artificial as the Hokusai woodcuts and Korin screens that had enthralled him as a schoolboy. Has any other poet, even Saint-John Perse, ever profited from such varied voyages?

His later poems reflect this huge widening of his experience. His memory as well as his imagination wings at the speed of light from one spectacle to a dozen others with analogous charms. Fountains Abbey, for example, evokes successively Zen monasteries in Kyoto, *artisanado* ceilings in Andalusia, and the Tiepolo in a Venetian church, where Dr. Burney (or was it perhaps the more susceptible Président de Brosses?) found a pretty nun

Conducting the choir and orchestra of orphan children,
with a sprig of pomegranate blossom
Tucked between her coif and her hair,

13

from whom our poet dashes off to recollections of Oporto,
Bavaria and Apulia. Often he harks back also to his
boyhood at Renishaw, where blackened miners tunnelled
for coal deep under the lake in the park, and his sister and
brother awoke their young sibling's love and also his
enthusiasms.

The newly-printed poems differ from his earlier work in
two respects: the rhymes he used to employ so happily are
now 'few, but roses' (often with roses as their subject); and
occasionally he expresses a new despair about the condition of humanity. 'What has come into and gone out of
the world within a lifetime!' Tyrannies have multiplied;
architecture has been replaced everywhere by mere building, such as the skyscrapers that manage to be both huge
and mean.

> For when young I was to net the Leonids
> But the world is not as I would have it.

Memories of his sister come to his rescue.

> The beauty and the poetry
> I learned from her
> Are antidotes to self-pity.

The self-pity she enables him to overcome springs not
from growing old but from the degradations he has lived
to witness.

All the three Sitwells began by puzzling or shocking
older critics with their modernity. Now Sir Sacheverell
seems to me the latest of our romantic poets—not the last,
because surely poets will again become romantic, just as
painters will again find inspiration, like their supreme
predecessors, in landscape, noble nudity and the personality revealed by human lineaments. Our feelings
about the beauty of Nature and the beauty of visual art
are far closer akin, I believe, than writers on aesthetics
have allowed. An apple-tree in blossom can bring much
the same sort of delight as the picture of one by Renoir;
and antelopes leaping in East African glades have en-
raptured my eye almost in the same way as Pisanello

14

drawings. Sir Sacheverell in his own words 'writes poetry for the sake of poetry, And for no other reason', and his poetry brims with the beauty he has sought for and worshipped, like the most devoted of pilgrims on the church-lined roads to Santiago de Compostella.

A Golden
Pheasant · *Kenneth Clark*

To recognise what we all owe to Sacheverell Sitwell, one must remember the state of art and letters in the early 1920's. It is a period that is now thought to have roared, with routs of ladies in low brimmed hats lurching out of the Eiffel Tower restaurant supporting their bearded Priapus; but its products were for the most part dismal and puritanical. In painting the dull purples and browns of Bloomsbury applied to a street-scene or a still-life; in poetry the Georgians and the thick, decent pages of *The London Mercury*; in architecture nothing between the heavy academism of Reggie Bloomfield and the arid, negative beginnings of functionalism. It was a world in which fantasy, richness and elaboration were completely excluded. Into this yard of virtuous fowls, laying their identical eggs, there strayed three golden pheasants—the Sitwells. They had begun by making friends with the most outrageous of all birds of plumage, D'Annunzio, and in the same year Sacheverell made his way to Naples and beyond. Baroque and Rococo were still terms of abuse, but in Rome and Vienna were just beginning to gain recognition. In Southern Italy they were considered vulgar beyond words. Yet such was the sureness of Sacheverell Sitwell's eye, and the persuasive eloquence of his prose, that in a single volume the whole was changed. *Southern Baroque Art* (1924) created a revolution in the history of English taste. The change was not confined to architecture. The music of Scarlatti, the singing of Farinelli, the *Commedia dell'Arte*, all these were part of the Sitwellian revolution.

The change was partly due to Sacheverell Sitwell's

quiet and unprejudiced response to things seen and heard, and partly to his style. Two years after *Southern Baroque Art* he published a book of digressions on the theme of recollected beauty, *All Summer in a Day*, which contains some of the finest passages of prose written in our day. It was the prose of a poet, and in fact he had already written a lot of poetry (fifteen volumes, he says in *Who's Who*, without naming them) totally unlike the short, anthologisable lyrics of the Georgians. In them he is still at his best in description, but can allow himself an even greater elaboration and a wider range of allusion. These poems, *Canons of Giant Art*, as one volume was appropriately called, always reminded me of Gothic tapestries, in which subtlety of design was at first hidden by a profusion of detail, although in the end the overall pattern was perceptible. And, sure enough, Sacheverell Sitwell soon turned his attention to those tapestries which his own writing so closely resembles, in a series of books called *The Gothick North*. His descriptions of tapestries are amongst the best things he ever wrote.

Sacheverell Sitwell is the most eager and rapid devourer of works of art I have ever known. In a gallery he could go all the way round and take me in the rear before I had finished with the first room. Yet he would have missed nothing and noticed a great deal that I would have overlooked. The result of this amazing speed of assimilation has been a series of journeys in search of new aesthetic experiences. Some have suited him better than others, and none better than Japan, which he described in one of the best of his post-war books, *The Bridge of the Brocade Sash*. How zestfully he saw the point of everything in that incomprehensible land, including many to which I had been blind. His eye is always alert. His appetite for the fantastic, the delicate and the bizarre never fails. What a marvellous travelling companion, if anyone could be found to keep up with him.

But this short note must not end with the suggestion that Sacheverell Sitwell was only a tireless observer of past civilisations. He found in his own time plenty to engage

17

his enthusiasm. He has a knowledge of music almost equal to his knowledge of architecture. He wrote brilliantly about Liszt, Scarlatti, Mozart and Bach, and part of William Walton's first symphony was composed in his house. He was a passionate student of old theatrical designs, and these two interests made him the friend of Diaghilev, whom he took to Hoxton to see Pollock's Juvenile Theatrical and Tinsel Warehouse. As a result he was commissioned to write the libretto for a ballet entitled *The Triumph of Neptune*: but the great impresario was already losing his grip, and allowed the magical images of the Tinsel Warehouse to be degraded by a second-rate painter named Pruna who, for some mysterious reason, had become fashionable. A splendid opportunity was lost.

In spite of his unequalled width of experience (and I mean unequalled, for surely no one else alive has seen and heard so many beautiful things in so many places, from Paris to Lagos) Sacheverell Sitwell has remained entirely consistent: a love of fantasy, of decorative invention and of glorious extravagance; and an imaginative understanding of how these can be made the substance of poetry. And, on the other side, a hatred of drabness and virtuous mediocrity.

The Palace of
the Muses · *Denys Sutton*

Men of letters prepared to comment on artists or artistic questions are more usually found on the Continent than in Great Britain. Among those who have done so in this country Hazlitt and W. E. Henley are two of the most successful. Other nineteenth-century writers attracted by the task include Thackeray, who penned some casual pieces, and George Moore, who fancied himself as an art critic and saw himself as the apostle of Impressionism. In our time Wyndham Lewis, artist, novelist and polemicist, published acute and forceful articles and books on art and Herbert Read, delicate poet of childhood and country, had an evangelical enthusiasm for modern art.

One contemporary writer whose talent is largely devoted to describing architecture and works of art is Sir Sacheverell Sitwell. A glance at the bibliography of his works published by Richard Fifoot (a revised edition has been issued recently) reveals that besides his special blend of art appreciation his fluent pen has produced poetry, travel-books, autobiography and short stories.

Now, a salvo is rightly being let off in his honour, and Neapolitan fireworks would be nice. He should be particularly fêted by the art world, for his pioneering activities in various directions have done much to alert the sensibilities of more than one generation to certain artistic subjects which, if now taken for granted, were barely known of, at any rate in this country, until his appearance on the scene.

Any assessment of his literary contribution as a whole, his poetry for example, would be out of place in this contribution. Yet, it deserves to be remembered that some of his verse has been inspired by artists such as Mantegna and Claude and works of art such as the Farnese Bull and the Hermes of Praxiteles, and that several of his early volumes of poetry contain decorations by Gino Severini, Wyndham Lewis, McKnight Kauffer and Rex Whistler.

Sitwell has never been a major writer about modern art, not from any hostility to the *avant-garde*, of which in his youth he was a champion, but because the opportunity to comment has not really come his way. His flair for what was significant in contemporary art was shown in 1919 when, together with his brother Osbert and Leopold Zborowski, and with the encouragement of Roger Fry, he collaborated in staging an exhibition of modern French art at the Mansard Gallery at Heal's in Tottenham Court Road. This important show, of which an account is provided by Sir Osbert Sitwell in his memoirs, presented a cross-section of the School of Paris and comprised works by Derain, Léger, Picasso and Soutine. It has a special claim to fame owing to its inclusion of paintings by Modigliani; it was apparently the first time that this artist's works were shown in London.

Picasso is Sitwell's main hero among painters and he considers him to be the artistic genius of the age. He awoke to his art in about 1919. If he and his brother had had their way, this master, rather than Severini, would have executed in 1921 or so the fresco decorations for Montegufoni, the castle of their father, Sir George Sitwell, outside Florence. As Sacheverell Sitwell wrote in *Cupid and the Jacaranda* (1952)

We had seen Picasso in this matter, the price was agreed, and there were to be painted balconies with musicians over the doors and two great scenes or landscapes with figures upon the walls composed, we were led to hope, in the Florentine manner, that is to say, under the influence of Botticelli, Benozzo Gozzoli, Alessio Baldovinetti.

Unfortunately their male parent and Picasso finally failed to settle the price of the commission, so what might well have turned out to be a masterpiece of decoration never materialised. Sitwell's particular preference is for Picasso's Blue and Rose periods, about which he has written with understanding, relating them to *Le Grand Gilles* of Watteau.

Sitwell's life as an aesthete started early; moreover, he went abroad with his parents, to Venice, Florence and elsewhere. A charming letter, written at the age of ten, to his brother Osbert reveals that he was already an embryonic globe-trotter with a special affection for architecture and a compulsive reader of guide-books. Sitwell was precocious, for while a schoolboy, he discovered Beckford (about whom he published an *opusculum* in 1930, now a rarity) and Flaubert's *Salammbô*. These writers account for much in his taste and style.

He must have been one of the few Etonians to have borrowed Fenellosa's *Epochs of Chinese and Japanese Art* from the school library and it is easy to understand his excitement when he was sent a copy of Wyndham Lewis's *Blast* with its references, among the lists of 'blast' and 'blessed', to Koêtsu, Kôrin and Sôtatsu. It was then that he nurtured the love of Japanese art and life—a latter-day version of eighteenth-century chinoiserie—that flowered in his book *Bridge of the Brocade Sash* (1959).

His interest in the ultra-modern was evident in his admiration for Marinetti, whom he corresponded with in 1915/16 when at Eton. He was also in touch with D'Annunzio, a writer he still admires. In 1920 he and his brother visited D'Annunzio at Fiume, when he was the hero of the hour, in the hope of persuading him to write an introduction to an edition of Rabelais in French and English (in Sir Thomas Urquhart's translation) with drawings by Picasso, a project that unfortunately proved abortive.

In the 1920s discussion in London artistic circles concerned with the Old Masters chiefly focused on the early Italians, for this was the period of Berenson and Duveen; or on the conventional portrait-painters of the English eighteenth century—those pictures of ladies with picture-

hats which appealed to the new rich in the United States·
The seventeenth- and eighteenth-century Italian Schools
were relatively unfamiliar, although they had been widely
collected in Great Britain in the past. Their works appealed to no more than a handful of connoisseurs; however, even before the First World War, Roger Fry acquired
Piazzetta's *The Sacrifice of Isaac*, now in the National
Gallery, London, and wrote the introduction to an exhibition of eighteenth-century Italian art at the Burlington
Fine Arts Club in 1911; Roberto Longhi and Hermann
Voss started to examine seventeenth-century Italian paintings and Martin S. Briggs published *In the Heel of Italy*
(1910).

The Seicento and Settecento obviously offered oppor-
tunities to a young man eager to make his mark and to
tackle unfashionable subjects. Sitwell was unusual in so
far as he could have easily then become one of the crowd
which settled in Paris; the 1920s was the epoch of the
Boeuf sur le Toit and a time when to be in Paris was to
be in the movement, as Clive Bell used to say. Of course,
the city delighted him and he enjoyed such privileges as
attending the first night of Stravinsky's *Pulcinella* on
15 May, 1920, and sitting in the same box as Boni de
Castellane and Picasso, who was responsible for the décor.
Yet it was a sign of his individuality that he struck out on
his own and found more to inspire him, as he himself said,
in Naples and Amalfi, than in the spires of Oxford or the
cafés of Montparnasse.

The Punchinello world of Naples sparked off his vision
of life and art. He saw it for the first time in the autumn
of 1920 after his visit to D'Annunzio with Osbert. Later
he recalled that he could never forget

. . . the excitement of discovering for myself the two long
narrow streets that traverse the old town with all their palaces
and churches: and the huge and wonderful old convent-
church of Santa Chiara with its majolica cloister, the ballroom of a church (as I remember it) with Sebastiano Conca's
ceiling painting of *David dancing and playing the harp before the
Ark*, the opera-boxes in its grand tier where the nuns looked

down through gilded lattices to join in the Mass, its air in general of an autocracy of noble nuns; or the Certosa di San Martino above the town, all flashing whiteness, white stucco, white marbles, even the one or two white-robed monks, with belvedere or balcony looking over the roofs of Naples across the bay to the smoking volcano and down again to the tenor voices, the carnations and mandolines of the modern town.

When Sitwell first came to this city it was well nigh impossible to find out anything about the contents of churches and he was lucky to come across Octavian Blewitt's *Guide to Naples* (1853) and the Abbé de Saint-Non's *Voyage Pittoresque au Royaume des Deux-Siciles* (1786), volumes which provided the backbone for his evocative passages on Naples, Caserta and elsewhere in his magical volume, *Southern Baroque Art* (1924).

One of his objectives in writing this book, he declared in the preface, was to substantiate his belief that 'there has been no age in history that is not worth examination, and that in the particular period I have chosen there are many qualities to be praised of which there is a total lack in our generation, for self-confidence and fluency are, surely, two qualities which no one could deny even to Luca Giordano'. Yet he did not seek to present a straightforward historical account of the artistic heritage of south Italy, for he writes:

My aim has been so thoroughly to soak myself in the emana-tions of the period, that I can produce, so far as my pen can aid me, the spirit and atmosphere of the time and place, without exposing too much the creaking joints of the machinery, the iron screws and pins of which are the birth dates and death dates of the figures discussed.

Rediscovery, revaluation and evocation; these have proved to be the driving forces behind his writing.

Southern Baroque Art was a pioneering effort with its praise for Solimena, Conca and Luca Giordano and it confirms Sitwell's insight that, in a later publication, *Monks, Nuns and Monasteries* (1963), he compares the last-mentioned painter to Donizetti and Rossini and maintains that all three were masters of improvisation. His lighthearted and impressionistic approach to Italian art has touches which are of his period, as when in *Southern Baroque Art* the still-lifes in the lower panels of the presses in inlaid and painted wood in the Certosa di San Martino are described as being as 'formal and complicated as the Cubists'. They show piles of books and vases of flowers, while generally there is a guitar lying among them that Picasso might have left there'.

In Sitwell's view, painters of sacred subjects of the late-sixteenth and early-seventeenth centuries were 'unable to represent anything more than the subject, alone and simply, that they were paid to portray. Anything like the emotion or the superstition of the large town population of say, Bologna or Naples is quite unrepresented. The fervour and the hysteria, with all its pagan accompani-ments of an un-Christian import, which were part of every religious festival, seem far away from the immaculate and perfectly executed works that the Carracci and their school produced.' However, for Sitwell, an element of this feeling crept into Italian art in Naples; he describes how the 'melodramatic realism of Caravaggio' was emulated in the south. Religious fervour was also dramatically evident in Spain with El Greco. Today there is nothing surprising about a writer enthusing over this master, but in the 1920s it was still a fresh thing to do, for only a decade or so earlier Charles Ricketts had been less than warm about him in his book on the Prado.

There is much that appeals in *Southern Baroque Art*, such as his account of the singing of the celebrated castrato Farinelli, who soothed the melancholy of Philip V in his palace at Aranjuez. Not the least attractive feature of the book is the appendix, which, for Sitwell's generation, must have seemed wondrously exciting with its references to Cimarosa, Pergolesi, Porpora and Vanvitelli, and to places such as Lecce, 'the Florence of Rococo art', as Gregorovius called it, and Noto, that superb Sicilian town of which Sitwell was the virtual discoverer and where there is now a restaurant called 'Le Sitwell'. In these years he enjoyed the opportunity of seeing buildings which have now either disappeared or fallen into disrepair, such as the fantastic Villa Palagonia. Sitwell's discoveries may well have helped to stimulate the adventurous buying by some American Museum men at this time, such as Chick Austen, the Director of the Wadsworth Atheneum, Hartford, Connecticut, who was a ballet- and music-lover and did much to make Americans aware of modern trends.

Sitwell played a vital part in founding the Magnasco Society; the two other main promoters were his brother Osbert and Tancred Borenius. This club held its first exhibition at Agnew's in 1924 and continued to arrange shows until 1928, with dinner parties and eighteenth-century music to mark the openings. Sitwell recalls that he knew the Venetian art-dealer Italico Brass, who bought pictures by Magnasco for some thirty years before identifying the artist by name, owning some fifty examples of his work; Campbell Dodgson, he remembers, did the same with Constantin Guy's drawings.

Before leaving Sitwell's role as a taste-maker for these then slumbering periods of Italian art, it should be mentioned that, like his brother, who shared his passion for the seventeenth and eighteenth centuries, he also admired the earlier Italian Schools. His appreciation of the great Florentine and Venetian masters is echoed in passages in his later books about his particular favourites, Benozzo Gozzoli, Bellini and Carpaccio.

In 1921 Sitwell underwent another revealing experience, for on a visit to the Salzburg music festival, he was enchanted by Austrian and southern German Baroque and Rococo. His book on the art and architecture of this region during these periods came out in 1927 and once again, although composed on a different scale from that of *Southern Baroque Art*, it was an eye-opener. Nowadays the grand architects of Central Europe, Fischer von Erlach, Lukas von Hildebrandt and J. B. Neumann, are familiar outside their countries of origin, but this was far from being so in the 1920s. Nor were painters such as Maulbertsch and Rottmayr known even to the most learned English pundits.

This volume may still be read with pleasure and even profit, although fresh material has come out since its appearance. In this book, as in others too, the author shows his knack of sketching in the background so that we may grasp the essentials of an historical situation and discover the nature of artistic cross-currents. He was lucky enough to see the theatrical drawings and costumes discovered in the Vienna Hofbibliothek after the 1914–18 War; they give 'convincing proof that the period of Leopold I was the Golden Age of theatrical production —that is to say, the Periclean and Shakespearean ages have their counterpart in this period of supreme representation'. And he sapiently noted that 'with this newly found knowledge we can see in the light of such men as Ottaviano Burnacini, or the Bibiena family, exactly how and why it was that Fischer von Erlach or Lukas von Hildebrandt was so swift and easy in his effects—how, to use a colloquialism, he got it across the footlights with such conspicuous freedom and brilliance'.

Even now, perhaps, Vienna's architectural eminence in the eighteenth century is not as widely reputed as it deserves. But Sitwell, writing about a city which had not yet suffered from the ravages of the Second World War, said, 'Vienna has more and better palaces of the kind than are to be seen in Rome, and the few still existing gardens are unique of their kind. Vienna is the only big city of that day with a commensurate building activity which can still be studied.' His account of German and Austrian architects and artists is lively and he makes stimulating allusions, comparing, for instance, the Zwinger in Dresden to the Paris International Exhibition and relating Permoser to Art Nouveau. What has to be remembered is that for an architectural writer at that date difficulties abounded when he was describing certain parts of Europe; for instance Sitwell stated that he was unable to secure photographs of any of those buildings in Hungary and Czechoslovakia that attracted him.

His love affair with the Baroque and Rococo was further revealed in *Spanish Baroque Art* (1924), a book which is not confined to Spain (which he first visited in April 1919) but which includes Portugal and the former Hispanic possessions overseas. He was breaking fresh ground as far as the English-speaking general reader was concerned and he drew attention to architects such as José Churriguerra and Pedro de Ribera, who were then scarcely known outside Spain. However, in this book his purpose was not to supply a detailed exercise in the history of art but to provide travellers with references to places they might miss. It would be easy, for instance, to leave Lisbon without having seen the marvellous chapel built to designs by Vanvitelli for João V in the church of São Roque—that luxurious jewel of Roman rococo craftsmanship to which he makes reference and which he wrote about again in his book on Portugal (1954).

Sitwell's passion in the 1920s for the Baroque and Rococo did not exclude a concern with the Gothic, probably on account of its elegance and spirit. His intriguing book *The Gothick North*, which appeared in three volumes between 1929 and 1931, is rich and ornate and includes some excellent passages of the descriptive writing which is his forte—an attempt to find equivalents in prose for his experiences. It reveals his passion for tapestries; he is one of the few non-specialist writers of our time who have treated this magical art form as it deserves, discovering in it a clue to the ethos of civilisations, and his skill in evoking mood is well displayed in his account of such famous series as the Pastrana or Hardwick tapestries, which possess an almost balletic quality.

The breadth of his interests at this time was considerable. Like many of the post-war generation, originality of entertainment delighted him: his sister Edith wrote the libretto for *Façade*, with music by William Walton and a backcloth by Frank Dobson, which was first performed privately in 1923. He was on close terms with this composer and also with Constant Lambert, who set to music his poem *Rio Grande*. The Russian Ballet, which he visited frequently, enthralled him and he became friends with Diaghilev; he tells us that one of this impresario's great enthusiasms was for Chabrier's *Le Roi Malgré Lui*. He describes in *Truffle Hunt* how he took Diaghilev down to Hoxton to see Pollock's Juvenile and Theatrical Tinsel Warehouse and a similar establishment run by H. J. Webb at the time when they were working and collecting material for the ballet *The Triumph of Neptune*. The libretto for this work was written by Sitwell himself and the music by Lord Berners; it was first performed on 3 December, 1926, at the Lyceum Theatre with Serge Lifar in a star role.

Few writers about art possess Sitwell's versatility and turn their attention to the other arts and Sitwell's range emerges in books or essays about Bach, Mozart, Scarlatti, Offenbach and Liszt. His volume on the last-mentioned composer is a full-scale affair which retains authority in musical circles. It is indicative of his compass that in his small book on Mozart (1932), which was castigated by Ernest Newman on its appearance, Sitwell argued that the composer's work may be related to the architecture of Fischer and Dietzenhofer, suggesting that the Amalien-burg recalls one of this composer's *divertimenti* or serenades. As to Scarlatti, he proposed that 'It is not, perhaps, invidious to see a similarity between Alexander Pope and Scarlatti'; both possessed, he claims, 'a caustic and sinister wit'. One of his most sustained and imaginative passages of musical interpretations is devoted to Bach's organ fugues: this is in *Splendours and Miseries* (1943).

Sitwell's love of Continental art might have led to his neglecting the British achievement, but this was not the case, and in the 1930s when inquiry into the national School was limited, he wrote about conversation and narrative pictures. It is worth pointing out that Sitwell's book on conversation pieces (1936) was dedicated to Sir Philip Sassoon, who in 1930 organised the famous exhibition of this *genre* at his Park Lane house, now the site of the Bunny Club. Sitwell's book owed much to that of his friend Dr. G. C. Williamson; since its publication fresh information has turned up, as may be seen from Ralph Edwards's volume on the subject. It is worth observing that in his volume Sitwell drew attention to photographs by Octavius Hill and Fox Talbot and showed himself to be in tune with the views of our day by warmly praising George Stubbs. In a passage comparing this artist with Zoffany he writes:

His [Zoffany's] paintings of skill, the *Tribuna* for instance, are trivial and laboured compared with the great *Whistlejacket*, or the frieze of mares and foals. Zoffany's painting of a room, hung with the masterpieces of the world and crowded with living men, is not a work of art when it is compared with a painting of horses in which there is not even a background. Zoffany had the gift of rendering, but not the genius of creating. Stubbs, in contrast to this, has a power to which all the cleverness of Zoffany can never attain. His is the only world of human beings; but that of Stubbs is Nature herself. Stubbs entered the different phases of his paintings from outside and did not, like Zoffany, paint them from within.

In his volume on narrative pictures (1937) Sitwell writes well about the little-known eighteenth-century artist Henry Walton, several of whose paintings, which have a touch of Chardin, were owned by his family, for one of his ancestors had been a friend of the artist. He also reveals his liking for Victorian art, of which the study was still in its infancy, although it had stalwart admirers such as Sitwell's friend Sickert, and in 1937 the Leicester Galleries held an exhibition of Victorian painting. An interesting section in the book deals with Richard Dadd, the parricide who was for years in Bedlam and one of whose mysterious works, *The Fairy Feller's Master-Stroke* (the Tate Gallery), then belonged to the poet Siegfried Sassoon. Sitwell's enthusiasm for George Cruikshank was marked; and he gave a Northcliffe Lecture about him in 1937, observing that this artist's *St. Cecilia's Day*, of 1837, depicts the sort of scene found in Stravinsky's ballet *Petrushka*, while, in *Early Morning* from *Sketches by Boz* (1837), 'No painting of Venice by Canaletto is more true to its subject than this small sheet of paper with its image of the greatest city of the world'. Another comic spirit he appreciates is John Leech.

Sitwell's concern with national art emerged forcibly in his well-known volume *British Architects and Craftsmen* (1945). This book, incidentally a best-seller, revealed his appetite for works of art of all sorts, plaster, ironwork, buildings and pictures and it helped to pave the way for the close study of seventeenth- and eighteenth-century British art which is such a notable feature of recent years. His praise for our heritage gains in conviction owing to his familiarity with foreign art.

Many observations about art and artists appear in such volumes of spiritual autobiography as *Dance of the Quick and the Dead, Sacred and Profane Love, The Hunters and the Hunted, Cupid and the Jacaranda*, to mention some of the most notable. These include excellent passages about Bosch and Bruegel, Picasso and Watteau and stress his imaginative approach to art. He takes us on a promenade of experiences through unfamiliar lands and subjects; and we never know where we shall land or what he will describe: for instance in *Splendours and Miseries* he indulges in a delightful comparison between the Spanish and the Viennese waltz. The passage is well worth quoting:

The *estudiantina* whirls and preens. It is the Spanish waltz; in the Spanish idiom of convention. The difference between the Viennese and Spanish waltz lies in the suggestion that the circles of the Viennese waltz expand outwards as do the ripples when a stone is dropped into a pond of water, while the Spanish waltz closes inward in rhythm. The Spanish rhythms contract and tighten and perhaps this is characteristic of Spain and its inhabitants. Of the burnt chocolate flavoured with cinnamon that they drink for breakfast, in contrast to the Danubian coffee and whipped cream; of their late hours and midnight music halls, of the spectacles of the bull fight and the *auto da fè*; of the garrotting of their criminals, who are bound to a post, in sitting position, holding a crucifix in their hands, while from the back, an iron collar is screwed tighter upon their necks to strangle them; of the stiff hoop of the little Infanta and the napkin she is holding in her blue-veined hand.

A particularly forceful imaginative foray is *Valse des Fleurs* (1941), subtitled *A Day in St. Petersburg and A Ball at the*

30

Winter Palace in 1868, which is a closely worked documentation of what life was like in old St. Petersburg: significantly it is dedicated to Cyril Beaumont, that learned historian of the ballet. Although Sitwell has never visited Russia, this effervescent book evokes the spirit of the Russian Court. Yet his affection for the haunting 'Valse des Fleurs' did not exclude compassion for the many inmates of Siberian prisons, or lead him to forget that four years before his chosen date the Polish rebellion was bloodily suppressed.

The British have an appetite for travel-books, the writing and reading of them. Sitwell, who is an expert at culling his material from earlier travellers, has devoted much of his skill to producing travel-books. There are volumes on Spain (1950) and Portugal (1954), countries he loves deeply, and on the Netherlands (1948) and Denmark (1956). Anyone interested in out-of-the-way information neglects these at his peril. Let us hasten to say that they are not regular guide-books, for, to take that on Spain, there is barely a mention of Madrid. All the same he gives the feel of the country and comments on aspects of it that might go unnoticed. The book on the Netherlands is typical of his method. Information is plentiful about the seventeenth century in Holland, the Golden Age, but what about the eighteenth century, the age of consolidation and quiet enjoyment of the riches garnered by the earlier generation? Little about Dutch art of the eighteenth century is available in English, or, for that matter, in Dutch, but many pertinent facts may be found in his volume. His account of the villas on the river Vecht and of the rococo and chinoiserie decorations of Friesland is original. In the same way there is no point in turning to his book on Denmark for a full-dress account of this lovable land. Yet he reminds us of the country's history, describes castles such as Ledreborg and introduces that intriguing painter Pilo, who, when he wrote about him, was known to few outside Scandinavia.

Bridge of the Brocade Sash (1959) is one of his most fascinating and attractive post-war travel-books, the result of a trip to Japan. In this vivacious record of a visit to a country that had always haunted him, Sitwell is at the top of his form, making amusing and valuable comments about daily life and scenery and providing an affectionate account of its buildings and works of art. This volume deserves to be treasured and, as usual, his comparisons are apposite, as in the relationship of a lacquer box for brushes and inkstones, showing a famous bridge by Kôetsu, to Art Nouveau: 'The whole conception of this curious object is one which in the Occident only the Catalan architect Gaudi could have designed.' His love of screen painting and of flowers and gardens comes across in this volume and his descriptive power is evidenced in his chapter on woodcuts:

It is probably only after having had the opportunity of seeing Japan with one's own eyes that some points concerning the *Ukiyô-e* and the art of Japanese woodcuts occur to mind. They are the truth to life of the woodcuts, and the reason why they annoy and irritate learned opinion in Japan. As to this latter point of view, which concerns the 'discovery' of Japanese woodcuts by Western painters and collectors in the middle of last century, it is very much as though 'serious' music lovers from Europe neglected concerts conducted by Toscanini and performances at the Metropolitan Opera House in New York and went instead to night haunts, there, and in Chicago and New Orleans, in order to study 'local music' on the spot. We hope to prove that there are even greater resemblances of fact in this suggested parallel. While, as to the first point raised, it is only necessary to sleep in a Japanese inn, or dine in a Japanese restaurant in order to see the accuracy of fact in the woodcuts, and this in spite of the factual improbability which is their outstanding charm to Western eyes.

Inevitably in later years Sitwell has tended to return to favourite themes. One instance of his *recherche du temps perdu* is *Southern Baroque Revisited* (1967), which contains some delightful memories of his visits to southern Europe, to Sicily in particular, and an account of Sir George and his man, Henry Moat, who has been immortalised by Osbert Sitwell. By the way, let us hope that Sacheverell

Sitwell will be persuaded to write his memoirs; he could tell us about Wyndham Lewis, who drew his portrait, Sickert, Constant Lambert and much else.

In the years since Sitwell published his first book on Baroque in the South additional facts have been uncovered; yet many of the buildings he saw have vanished or declined in their station in life. This book will afford pleasure to any admirer of the eighteenth century; it contains a spirited account of Tiepolo and Scarlatti, illustrating a portrait of the latter, and an acute chapter on Borromini, Guarini, Juvarra and Vittone, as well as one on Spain. One of the most agreeable sections deals with the *Estilo Mexicano*, in which observations about art and architecture, based on three visits to Mexico, are combined with recollections. He declares that more than once R. B. Cunninghame Graham told him of 'how as a young man he would swim his horse across the Rio Grande just to sleep in Mexico!'

When writing about Mexico in the 1920s he had never been there; however, his imagination had been fired as a child by reading John Stephens's *Incidents of Travel in Central America, Chiapas and Yucatan* (1841), which he had chanced upon in his grandmother's library when eight or nine years of age, 'with Catherwood's mysterious and wonderful drawings of the stone pyramids and carved monoliths of the Mayans'. In the early days, he says, there was little to refer to for the reconstruction of Mexico's past: Baxter's *Spanish Colonial Architecture* was one source and Terry's *Guide to Mexico* another, 'so progress was achieved more through poetic licence than dull fact'.

Sitwell, who belongs to the age of the traveller rather than to that of the tourist, has been able to write about Latin America at length, not only in *Southern Baroque Revisited*, but in *Golden Wall and Mirador* (1961), which is based on the visit he and his wife paid to Peru. This contains typically evocative and perceptive accounts of buildings and works of art and renders the atmosphere of the country and of such places as Lima, Cuzco, the ancient Inca capital, and Macchu Picchu. The last-named was the secret city of the Incas and was only rediscovered in 1911. Although specialists such as George Kubler and H. E. Wethey have published volumes dealing with various aspects of Peruvian art and architecture, it is never easy for the general reader to secure an insight into them, and Sitwell's book provides an agreeable contribution to the subject. It gains in interest for its reproduction of the paintings of J. M. Rugendas, the German painter who left such amusing pictures of Lima in the first half of last century. One of the most appealing plates in the book is J. Wayne's water-colour *A street scene in Lima, showing wooden miradors*, which dates from 1835 and could serve as a backcloth for a ballet.

Recent years have witnessed little abatement in Sitwell's output. In the lengthy book *Monks, Nuns and Monasteries* he makes many good points, such as that South German Rococo, rather than Victorian Gothic, is the true descendant of medieval art; though he affirms that St. Gallen is 'quite empty of emotion, with no distinguishing features, too well cared for as if by a brigade of hoovers'. He also produced a survey, *Gothic Europe* (1969), which reveals his love of British cathedrals and churches and, typically, it includes a chapter on the Manoelino style and one on tapestries which are 'a pawn to mystery'.

'Tuppence-coloured' rather than 'penny-plain' has always appealed to Sitwell. He sees the world as a stage: harlequinade, ballet, theatre, opera, have enchanted him, the world as illusion, in fact. He has always loved things and experiences gay and charming, and he is enchanted by fragrant soaps, roses, exotic flowers and richly plumaged birds. One of his most cadenced prose passages occurs in his introduction to *Fine Bird Books* (1953). An insight into his taste, especially his love of the unusual and response to all that induces nostalgia or is evocative, may be found in his volume of snippets, *Truffle Hunt* (1953), partly composed of pieces contributed to the *Sunday Times*; this makes a splendid and informative bedside book and has amusing illustrations.

In the mind's eye Sitwell may be seen in the British

Museum Reading Room where he has been an assiduous reader since 1917, or in some leather-scented country-house library turning over elephant-folios on a hunt for unusual illustrations that will permit him to bring back to life 'the aristocracy of the dead'. His type of writing, in which the stops are usually pulled out, may not be all that fashionable today. He is not a writer who lays down the law; he only seeks to convey the sensations that have given him pleasure. Those intent only on securing precise information and adverse to mandarin prose may not respond to Sitwell's books; on the other hand, those sharing his love of the 'rare and curious' can become addicted to them. Such readers appreciate his enthusiasm, life-enhancement and ability to discern piquant and unusual subjects; he has the gift, too, of making us feel that the world's our oyster. He is the man for those who have no objection to '*La vie en rose*'.

Sitwell's vision of art and of life has always been that of the poet and it is the poetical quality of his writing allied to his sense of style and enthusiasm that makes the communication of his visual experiences so important and appealing.

Shall These
Bones Live? · *John Smith*

Almost forty years ago, Duckworth published the *Collected Poems* of Sacheverell Sitwell; but even in 1936 they formed a fat book of nearly six hundred pages of fairly small print. Since then the author has published only the occasional poem privately or in magazines—not more than half a dozen or so. That is not because he has stopped writing them; there exist in MS more than three hundred, and a selection has been published semi-privately.

Of the three famous writing members of the Sitwell family, his name, and possibly his work, is much less well known than that of Osbert or Edith yet he is in many ways a more interesting writer than either. His range is enormous. He writes, and one has ample evidence of the truth of the statement:

It is my belief that I have informed myself of nearly all works of art in the known world. I cannot think that anything considerable is missing. Where I have not been in person, I have read and studied. I have heard most of the music of the world, and seen nearly all the paintings. But, in order to create, it is necessary to remember it all with one part of the mind, and forget it with the other.*

The last sentence is admirable, though I am not so sure, from the evidence of the bulk of his poetry, that he has entirely succeeded in following his own maxim, for sometimes the sheer weight of knowledge, of information, does get in the way of complete success.

It is not that he is esoterically allusive. There are none

* *Journey To The Ends of Time*, Cassell, 1959.

of the complexities that are to be found in the work of Eliot or Pound. He does not use so exacting a shorthand as these two poets; his style is more expansive, his manner more discursive. Where the knowledge intrudes is in the feeling the reader often has of the poet choosing the subject on which to write, rather than allowing the subject to impose itself on his imagination and force its utterance through an emotional necessity. This would have seemed less of a criticism in the nineteenth century, for the professional man of letters, in which the poet was allowed, was *supposed* to be engaged in the production of art as a working activity. Although it was required that the god should speak to him he was not allowed to sit back and wait hopefully for the miraculous voice. That Sacheverell Sitwell has worked is evident in the list of no less than seventy-seven books given at the front of the first volume (the second has not yet appeared) of *Journey to the Ends of Time*. The sheer professionalism is unnerving. But has the god spoken? Undoubtedly, yes.

The pattern of his working life is not unlike that of Walter Savage Landor; both have written prose works treating at great length subjects of a philosophical or artistic nature, while concurrently exploring similar themes in their poetry. Occasionally, as with Landor, it is possible to discover a greater poetic sensibility and a greater subtlety of language in the prose exploration than in the poem. There is perhaps a reason for this; fascinated as he is by Baroque Art he uses most skilfully one of the major elements of that style: decoration. Poetry is less amenable to decorative features than prose—that is if it is to be real poetry and not attractive verse, or rhetoric. But if sometimes he is unable to make poetry out of the prose material of some of his subjects, he is often able to write passages of prose of such refinement, of such grandeur, of such philosophical profundity, as to transform those pages into near poetry. Certainly he has the most superb gift of re-creating a place and a time so that we do not merely know what it might have been like in fact, but can discover its spiritual essence, can feel the resonances of its inner life

and detect the kind of breath that animated it and produced through its people the especial, personal art and
way of life. To read *Southern Baroque Art* is almost to enjoy
that world at first hand, so vividly is it brought to life.

But what of the poems? The *Collected Poems* (from which
all my quotations are taken) is prefaced by a long and in
some ways disastrous essay by Edith Sitwell. She properly
says that their blood relationship should be no barrier to
her writing such an introduction, and she has many
pertinent things to say about poetry in general and
Sacheverell Sitwell's poetry in particular; but for the
general reader, even the avid reader of poetry, the long
discussion of the excellence of the poet's technique is
repetitious and boring, though she does show how remarkable his craftmanship is. Sacheverell's own modest preface
gives perhaps a clearer insight into the nature of many of
the poems. He writes: 'These poems were written to give
(*her*) pleasure and this must be, at once, their excuse and
recommendation.' Many critics might pounce on the use
of the word 'pleasure'; but to give pleasure is not a bad
aim, after all—and indeed what work of art does not do
this in some manner or another?

The first poem, *Outskirts*, has about it a slightly uneasy
modern air; uneasy because it is neither in the world of
twentieth-century urban disillusionment nor yet still in the
more comfortable romantic world of the middle victorian
poets. There are lines which are close enough to Eliot to
make one reflect that in this manner Eliot is the finer poet;
he inhabits more surely one world.

> And here disposed upon the grass, I see
> Confetti-thick the amorous couples—

or later:

> Beneath them, where the river winds,
> You hear the spurting of a gramophone—
> A fountain playing with discoloured water;
> And the strumming of a piano,
> Too far for voice to carry,
> Jerks like a mote before our eyes.

There is a kind of self-conscious newness about this, and about many of the poems in the early collections, that irritates not because of any introduced slickness but because one feels that the poet is not speaking in his proper voice; there is also a certain air of condescension in the tone and the references to things and to people. One is too aware of the 'superior poet' to feel properly at ease.

Gradually the self-consciousness disappears, but for a long time in its place is introduced a decorative element and a discursiveness that prevents the poems from standing up clear and bold in their own right. He lacks the audacity of Yeats in the dramatic lyric, or the intellectual rigour of Eliot, or the lyrical grace of Hardy. Indeed he suffers from the gravest problem of the romantic poet, who in the lyric can be so easily seduced away from simple eloquence by a prettiness of language. It is rare that the purely descriptive lyric succeeds as anything more than an attractive exercise in the chosen formal manner; however little it becomes explicit there is always the necessity for a powerful emotional core, for the lyric in fact to *be* something rather than to *describe* something. Sacheverell Sitwell's early lyrics are too often marred, on reflection, by the realisation that they have been elegant glosses on some aspect of the visible world and have rarely penetrated beneath the surface to reveal a possible essence, a possible meaning. Nevertheless, though they are kept rather rigidly at this level they are fastidiously written and dexterously maintained. The group of ten *Serenades* shows how admirably he can play the game proposed by, and for, himself. They are less witty, less audacious, less sheerly preposterous than the majority of Edith Sitwell's poems in, say, *Façade*, and they are inclined to be a little too embedded in a past age:

> Answer again, you burning streams,
> Nor bend your flame, nor melt your snows;
> It is not only straw that burns
> To feel the hot sun look on it,
> And every phoenix is not dead.
>
> *Serenades: II*

39

But as he begins to move toward the more complex poem of some length, usually related to a subject from the past, a new strength becomes apparent. Using the short line in many of the lyrics, there is a tendency for them to become too lightweight, and to appear somewhat facile; and when, as is often the case, a longer line is interspersed, it seems to bring with it an element of prose that sits uneasily within the poetic framework. With the longer poems of his 'middle period' the extended rhythms, the ability to hold a melodic line throughout a complete stanza, add a gravity that seems more appropriate to his curiously enquiring mind. The growth is slow, and on the whole success still eludes him. One senses that he is moving toward something, but that not only has he not yet reached it, but perhaps does not even know what it is. Gradually, though, we begin to perceive that often where the language and the thought is most firmly manipulated the theme is some exploration or reflection upon death. Somewhere, somehow, the poet has become obsessed with the thought that the dead are merely dead. That is all.

The first section of *The Thirteenth Caesar*, entitled *The Opening of the Tomb*, moves exploratively into this territory of death:

'Tis pity they are ashes!
Could we but find their bodies,
Opening the porphyry to see those sores within it,
We'd unroll the league long bandages
And rub their bones with salt. . . .

In this poem, also, he uses a device which has a permanent attraction for him: the introduction into a classical theme of an image from the present—the photographer. Let us fix this in a photograph, he seems to say, and then we can examine it. He is not as specific as that, but the mere introduction into the mind of the reader of this figure of the photographer sets up a reverberation which induces a willingness to look at the subject in detail. Here, too, he begins to explore an intellectual idea in greater depth; there is more argument—or perhaps the argument is more clearly exposed—and the decorative nature of the language is used to heighten an awareness of the theme, rather than to stifle it in a proliferation of flowers and leaves.

His appetite now seems whetted for an attempt at a really big poem, and after some delightful musical pieces—including *By the Rio Grande* (which was indeed set to music by Constant Lambert)—he embarks on his long poem *Dr. Donne and Gargantua*. This, in six elaborate Cantos, is a strange mixture of comedy, drama, straight narrative, philosophical disquisition and mystical exploration. It is, I think, only fitfully successful. It is lacking in incisiveness. It fails to engage the reader in the main purpose of its argument, though that argument is in itself fascinating—the conflict (as particularised in the figures of Donne and Gargantua) between the world of the real, gross substance, and the metaphysical world. Which is the more important? What does God intend, what does He reveal; how important is He, indeed, in a world changed by the thoughts as well as the actions of man? Or must the world of necessity exist in this double state? But one longs for a simpler statement of the problem. The characters too often get in the way of the game itself. However, as can often happen, the expansion in a longer poem with a reasonably dramatic framework can produce in subsequent lyrics an ease as well as a strength which was not there before. This is certainly the case in the work of Sacheverell Sitwell and there are some deft and charming lyrics leading up to the poem *Exalt the Eglantine*. They are still overburdened, however, with luxurious images and slightly self-indulgent longings; the fruits are always luscious, the sun and air extravagantly golden, the world honeyed and cloying. This attempt to push through into an idyllic landscape of pastoral ease and leisure finally produces not so much a delightful languor as a sense of *ennui*.

It is necessary to remind ourselves, though, that some of these considerations are brought about by the particular time in which we live, and the dominant fashion within

the various arts. Just as some artists seem vivid within
their own time but fade as the conditions of that time
change, so some artists can only be seen clearly when they
have, as it were, assumed the stature of classic figures, and
such features as historical relevance become not less important, but are viewed within a more expansive time
scale. A poet of the heroic traditional approach of Mr.
Sitwell can be criticised for writing out of the subject of
poetry, rather than out of the immediate engagement and
struggles of contemporary man; but this criticism can be
laid at the door of many poets who hold a firm place in
the English tradition. Where Eliot can say, succinctly,
These fragments I have shored against my ruins, Sacheverell
Sitwell dwells on the fragments, those glories of the Euro-
pean or occasionally Eastern past, and leads us into a
consideration of civilisations and endeavours often strange,
often bizarre, often greatly exalted, but offering in their
diversity and grandeur a comment on our own fragmented
age. The most valuable experiences of his life would seem
to be those related to art—to painting, poetry, music,
sculpture, which at times he prizes more highly than the
people who brought those works into being. In this he is
not dissimilar to Yeats, who could state so emphatically:

> Once out of nature I shall never take
> My bodily form from any natural thing,
> But such a form as Grecian goldsmiths make
> Of hammered gold and gold enamelling. . . .*

Significantly, then, his stature as a poet is tremendously
enhanced by the poems which make up his last published
book: *Canons of Giant Art*, subtitled *Twenty Torsos in Heroic
Landscapes*. This is no slim volume of 'contemporary poetry'
but a substantial book of poems on far-ranging themes
pursued at considerable length. Suddenly Sacheverell
Sitwell finds his true subject matter, and that subject
matter forces him to the discovery of his extraordinarily
personal style. It is a majestic style in keeping with the
themes he presents, and those themes are firmly placed

* W. B. Yeats, *Sailing to Byzantium*.

within the heroic virtues of man; there is no space in these poems for what he construes as the trivia of the common man's day-to-day activities—these are poems about heroes, and the heroes are addressed in a high and magnificent manner. It is truly within this world that Sacheverell Sitwell finds the proper inspiration for his greatest work. He has not the gift of Edward Thomas or Philip Larkin to expose in small, beautifully manipulated lyrics the soul beneath the flesh of the average modern man. He could never have had a hand in the production, either, of the *Bayeux Tapestry*, but might happily have contributed to *The Lady with the Unicorn*.

He ransacks the artistic storehouse of the past for themes of heroism, dedication, death, love, ritual, and in doing so brings forth a group of poems as remarkable as they are currently underestimated. The series opens on a majestic note with *Fugal Siege* (in the manner of Mantegna) and includes poems whose inspiration are drawn from subjects as far apart as the two golden cups of Vaphio in the Athens Museum, the *Royal Hunt and Storm in the Forest* from Berlioz's opera *The Trojans*, *Krishna with the Milkmaids*, and, especially, *Agamemnon's Tomb*. This last is a poem of resonant splendour. Against its controlled grandeur many much-vaunted works look very small beer indeed. In this great poem Sacheverell Sitwell finds exactly the subject his mind demands, and he writes with heroic gravity (if the phrase is permissible) in a style that is flexible enough to encompass tenderness, passion and despair, and to culminate in a calm and resolute manner that is appropriate to the somewhat stoical conclusion.

In this poem the praise given him in the preface by Edith Sitwell is well justified, for indeed the sheer craftmanship is staggering. The language swells, modulates, pauses, drops, as the theme is stated, developed, recapitulated and resolved in a kind of Bachian magnificence.

    Tomb
    A hollow hateful word
    A bell, a leaden bell the dry lips mock,

Though the word is as mud or clay in its own sound
A hollow noise that echoes its own emptiness,
Such is this thing, this cell to hold the box.

We are at once plunged into the poem, which continues
its examination of the desolateness of death through a
consideration that human beings cannot think for a long
time about it, for if they did the subject would be so
obsessing that they would be able to think of nothing else.
This leads to the ordinary thought, expressed many times
by many people, but never with greater intensity, that
rich and poor are alike in death, and that so many
millions have died it is astonishing that there is any place
left at all for the living. The pace is heavy, the thought
implacable, but it leads to a most tender and exquisite
short passage introducing a more personalised note:

Now it was so little that a babe was more,
No more of self, a little feeble thing
That love could not help,
That none could love for what it was;
It looked, and Love saw it, but it could not answer;
Life's mystery was finished, only death was clear. . . .

All this is a general consideration of the subject matter;
the exploration of the tomb as a place, anywhere, to which
we all must come. But now the poem moves to the
particular, and as it does so different thoughts come in.
This is not, after all, *any* tomb; it is the tomb of Agamemnon at Mycenae. The bridge from the general to the
particular is organised and built with great imaginative
dexterity:

All is degradation in the chambers of dead bones,
Not marble, nor porphyry, but make it worse
For the mind sees, inside it, to the stained wet shroud
Where all else is dry, and only that is fluid,
So are carven tombs in the core to their cool marble,
The hollowed out heart of it, the inner cell,
All is degradation in the halls of the dead;
I never thought other things of death, until
The climb to Mycenae. . . .

44

And he concludes the passage with admirable dramatic effect as he confronts us with the object:

> The wind shrieked, the rain poured, the steep wet stones
> Were a cliff in a whirlwind, by a raging sea,
> Hidden by the rainstorm pelting down from heaven
> To that hollow valley loud with melancholy;
> But the dark hill opened. And it was the tomb.

The difficulty with this sort of poem lies precisely in the confronting of the principal object; after many splendid introductions, how often have we not been let down by the revelation? But not here. The introspection, the reflection on the subject of the finality of death which has been pursued with such skill, is now replaced with the most wonderful and evocative description of the tomb itself. The style remains the same, but the tone is lightened; and from such an accumulation of images of horror or distress grows an andante-like movement of exquisite loveliness describing how within the tomb Agamemnon lay while the bees brought in honey, filling the cavity with a substitute summer. But it did nothing to alter his predicament:

> How sweet such death, with honey from the flowers,
> A little air, a little light, and drone of wings,
> To long monotony, to prison of the tomb!
> But he did not know it. His bones, picked clean,
> Were any other bones. The trick is in our minds: . . .

Visiting the same place in a later year he finds things unchanged, but briefly allows a little flicker of hope to grow up, and asks Agamemnon to tell him of the mysteries of death—not from the tomb, but from the Castalian spring. In some way perhaps the dead live on in the places they have somehow made their own. But for themselves there is no chance of resurrection:

You are dead, you are dead, and all the dead are nothing to us,
There's nothing, nothing, nothing, not a breath beyond:
O give up every hope of it, we'll wake no more,
We are the world and it will end with us:
The heart is not a clock, it will not wind again,

The dead are but dead, there is no use for them,
They neither care, nor care not, they are only dead.

Certainly it is a conceit, and perhaps a fairly baroque
one at that, to say that after all Agamemnon did speak to
Sacheverell Sitwell at the Muse's fountain. The poem is a
great inspiration, and must surely be seen, in the long run,
as one of the finest poems of some length written in English
in our time.

Sacheverell Sitwell
Revalued · *Leonard Clark*

The work, or at least the names, of Sir Osbert, Edith and Sacheverell Sitwell first became widely known in the 1920's, though each of them had published books before that period. They began their literary careers as poets, and though each has written much prose, especially the brothers, they remained faithful to poetry. Because of their attitude towards Philistinism and unsympathetic critics, and because they were pioneers, both in arts and letters, they did not suffer from the obscurity which, otherwise, they might, together and singly, have experienced. These 'poor young people', as they once called themselves, seemed to represent in their writings and actual lives the various aesthetic changes which were taking place in English thought and fashion after the 1914–1918 war. Because they regarded poetry as an art which demanded brilliant verbal and rhythmic technique for its success, and because they believed in an Apollo-like interpretation of all the arts, they gathered to themselves a number of intellectuals who, with them, were anxious to sweep away the last vestiges of all that was mean and ugly in late Victorian life. They wanted to think of life as being lived freshly, imaginatively, decoratively and daringly.

It is not surprising, therefore, that their modes of expression of these things were attacked and ridiculed. They were dubbed 'precious', 'insubstantial aesthetes', and even 'frauds' by those who did not understand what they were trying to do, say and be. Fortunately, many of their early supporters have remained true to them, and to their ideals.

At one time it was customary to lump them all together.

They were known as 'the Sitwells', as if they were a kind of ailment. They had invented 'Sitwellism', a by-product, many thought, of Cubism, Dadaism and, of course, lunacy. They were given the literary form of a golden-headed hydra, and they were considered a kind of intellectualised Cerberus. But as Sir Osbert, Edith and Sacheverell Sitwell grew older, and the excitement of the 1920's died down, it was discovered, what indeed was always the case, that their work is individual and that each is different from the others. Naturally they are all Sitwells, which means that they have common traditions and a common up-bringing. All of them revered the arts and all of them abhorred the insincere, the ineffectual and the ugly.

The work of Sacheverell Sitwell, the youngest member of this trinity, has hardly received the attention it deserves. It is thought that this is due to the development of his sister as a poet, and to his brother as a stylish and, on occasions, satirical compiler of autobiographies. The light of publicity has tended to fall on them though at no time has it failed to cast some beams on him. But Sacheverell Sitwell is a writer of considerable merit. Although his poetry lacks much of the religious and mystic passion of his sister and the wit and nostalgia of his brother, they do not possess, to the same extent, his purity of utterance or his beautifully woven poetic line. She was forced by sorrow, and by a heart that reached out to warm all creatures, to wander among the unhappinesses of the world, and to offer a balm as cooling as Gilead, and a hope divinely given. Sir Osbert, thinking of the life of the past, returned to the happier avenues of the England of his childhood. Sacheverell hides his deepest feelings in a cloud of sublime detachment, but releases stupendous thoughts. Nevertheless, he has never allowed himself to be completely disillusioned and cares as deeply as any for the good and beautiful.

Between them, the Sitwells represent a miniature *Encyclopaedia Britannica*, but it is Sacheverell who has explored the minor roads of knowledge. He has laid bare more obscurities to the naked sky than either his brother or sister; he has resurrected half-a-dozen or so warm corpses from a score of sleeping centuries. He is the authentic scholar, patient, thorough, questing. Few living English writers have revealed so many hidden and forgotten jewels in literature, painting and architecture. Prose has only been his working medium when poetry would have made things more difficult for his readers.

In addition to his poems, which include the fantastic *Dr. Donne and Gargantua*, the fragrant *Hortus Conclucus* and the massive *Canons of Giant Art*, Sacheverell Sitwell has covered a vast field of knowledge in his prose work. Music, ballet, travel, costume and flowers have also fascinated him. As a very young man, he published *Southern Baroque Art* and *German Baroque Art*, books which created such a sensation at the time that, ever since, it has been the fashion to associate him only with the baroque and to see its influences in all his writings. It has been too often forgotten that he has written very much more about matters not connected with the baroque.

The unusual and the little-known fact seem to attract this civilised, cultured scholar most of all. He has found beauty in the Netherlands, in the Orient, in Edinburgh as well as in Spain, Paris and English country houses. He possesses an imagination of amazing power and clarity, which can be fired not only by large tracts of unknown territory, but also, like Bewick and Clare, can seize upon the details within that territory, put them under the microscope and permit all their facets, both factual and fanciful, to shine. The larger territory, which he has so often explored, is a veritable *divertissement*. As the coloured pictures move round to the motion of his hand, it is seen that they are Beckford, Mozart, Massine, Fabergé and Cupid. British architects rub shoulders with poltergeists. Audubon's *American Birds* take their curious place in Victorian galleries of fashion. The Sleeping Beauty slumbers among old-fashioned flowers, porcelain figures and domestic portraits.

Sacheverell Sitwell does not often stoop to gaze upon the drab colours of a mechanical and repetitive age.

Because he wishes for all to share in beauty, he wanders with stars, quizzes tropical birds, lives *La Vie Parisienne*, and gathers perpetually nosegays of iris, lilies and roses. All that is decorative, fascinating to touch, odd in texture or radiant with colour, appeals to him and feeds his imagination. In some ways he is the Phoebus of twentieth-century writing, all silver and gold, velvet and plush, noonday sun and midnight moon, using words as Cellini used silver.

His imagination is so fertile that almost anything can set it in motion. One line from Nietzsche produced *Two Variations on Themes out of Zarathustra*. The closing lines of *The Dunciad* were sufficient to create *Actor Rehearsing*. He hears the Santander Quartet at a concert of Spanish music, and then proceeds to compose a series of poems with the authentic feeling and atmosphere of Spanish wineshops, fortune tellers, gipsies and village bands. The *Comendador* is there, and cowled nuns in their whispering convents. This ranging imagination is soaked in classical mythology but there has also passed through it the cultures of India, Russia and Mexico. What it produces on paper seems to take on the innermost qualities of what is being described and delineated. Over and over again one is reminded of what Gerard Manley Hopkins called *Inscape*. John Donne's

> *Go, and catch a falling star,*
> *Get with child a mandrake root*

gave birth to the first canto of 'Dr. Donne and Gargantua'. There are endless examples of this method of poetic composition, one deep calling to another. It is not an unusual method; it is part of the tradition of literature. But what the imagination of Sacheverell Sitwell conceives is particularly magical and breathtaking. With himself as the pivot, he has thrown out a huge caliper point and enclosed concentric circle with concentric circle. Everything seems to be fair game. Pope and Donne have often been his mainsprings; so have Greene, Marlowe, Lyly and Peele. William Browne, of Tavistock, does not know that he was

Portrait of Sacheverell Sitwell by Christopher Angeloglou

responsible, nearly 400 years later, for enchanting poems by Sacheverell Sitwell about mulberries, apples and quinces. Loveliness is created out of loveliness, and is preserved for those who would share it.

Only rarely does Sacheverell Sitwell recall by name that small circle of England which cradled him. But bluebells in Derbyshire, a stone Venus at Bolsover Castle, and the woods at Eckington have been enough to recapture, for other eyes than his, the mists at Renishaw and the collieries in rainwashed trees. Of the woods at Eckington, he writes, remembering his childhood,

The miller and his wife have gone;
The cockerel at his fanfare to their last march of sun
Stood on that stone bridge, the highest station for his watch,
And was moved in a hen coop before the sun rose high;
Yet, remembering the collieries,
The noise of a giant forge hid in the trees,
I knew that this bridge led to a pit in the deep woods,
A pit with slanted galleries before they sank real shafts,
And the coal waggons rumbled on that high thin arch
By the mill stream that worked in great thickets of the
    yellow corn
Crushing out their life into a white bread for men;
Their two paths crossing, their lives led side by side,
Like the nettles and the campion in this summer wood.
By now the 'lords and ladies' in their green hoods
Nod near to sleep,
The coal pit and the mill are dead, the corn lands are stubble,
But the nettles still hold wine for goats, and the campion
    stands sentinel
Holding the summer wood for ghostly trumpet and black
    shapes of shadow.

This is not obscure poetry, the work of a clouded mind, the rambling fancies of an 'insubstantial aesthete'.

When he sees an unknown name scratched upon a window, he writes three mirror poems and, as the letters spelling the name bite into his consciousness, he asks

Or were the shining fences of the rain pitched there?
Did fruit like a lodestone hang outside the window . . .

His *Canons of Giant Art: Twenty Torsos in Heroic Landscapes* is one of the longest poems in the language, but it all resulted from what he had seen and remembered in other arts. He chose, for instance, paintings by Mantegna and Claude, two golden cups in the museum at Athens, an opera by Berlioz, Greek and Indian fables, the Hermes of Praxiteles, and the poetry of Dante, all great and memorable expressions of man's love of beauty, and constructed round them an equally giant and detailed poem. The opening lines of Canto 5 of this poem, called *Agamemnon's Tomb* (as seen at Mycenae) embody the very essence of an awe-inspiring subject.

Tomb
A hollow hateful word
A bell, a leaden bell the dry lips mock,
Though the word is as mud or clay in its sound;
A hollow noise that echoes its own emptiness,
Such is this awful thing, this cell to hold the box.
It is breathless, a sink of damp and mould, that's all,
Where bones make dust and move not otherwise;
Who lives the spider or the worm, for this,
That they starve in there, but are its liveliness?
The gravecloth, coldest and last nightgown,
That's worn forever till its rags are gone,
This comes at the end when every limb is straight,
When mouth and eyes are shut in mockery of sleep.
Much comes before this, for the miser hand
That clutches at an edge of wood, a chair, a table,
Must have its fingers broken, have its bones cracked back,
It's the rigor mortis, death struggles out of life,
A wrestling at the world's edge for which way to go.

Sacheverell Sitwell is not always an easy poet to understand and he certainly demands a high degree of intelligence in his readers. This was also true of Donne, Browning and Hopkins and, in our own day, of Dylan Thomas and T. S. Eliot. But Sacheverell Sitwell is never only difficult; there is much more to his work than mere cerebration. His poems are felt as well as made, and many of them have been deeply experienced in the world in which their writer legitimately wanders. He does not belong to any schools of poetry, he is neither political nor propagandist, and his poetic technique, though original in its rhythmic power, has developed out of authentic English traditions. His ability to create visual images that are full of light, colour and truth, is impressive. He speaks of 'the cindered sun', 'the nightingale's black livery of death', 'oaten tragedies against the leaden window', and of 'an Indian temple tethered in a mangrove shade'. It is true that, at times, he is too prodigal with his images, so that his least successful poems, in his own words 'creak under pyramids of grapes'; but these are the blemishes one would expect from a poet who writes on so large a scale. The purity of his detachment generally sees him through and serves as a bulwark against tedium.

Although Sacheverell Sitwell can get to the heart of things, he paints his pictures from afar. With his eye clearly on the object and his ear ready to receive every overtone, he works like a Titian or Beethoven. He has succeeded in fusing a tremendous range of colour with an equally tremendous range of sound. And this is because he has a superb poetic ear. He does not disdain to use rhyme, but he can produce other echoes, because of his command of assonance and dissonance. He knows how to change and shift vowels, vary rhythms, give pauses and, indeed, to give the essential texture to a poem.

His prose works are the logical extensions of his poetry. They represent his desire to write himself out and much could be written about their stylish language and their treasure stores of knowledge. It has never been very easy to pin him down or classify him. He remains gazing on mountains with eagle eyes, though sharing with others the burning glory of his noonday sun and midnight moon. Maybe he has told us most about himself in the poem called *A March Past at the Pyramids*, which has these lines:

My natural clumsiness could not prevent
More abstract knowledge, and an obvious bent
For things that carry motion to a pitch

Where only calculation, with its stitch
Of makebelief, and taking things for granted,
Completes the web, and leaves the answer planted
As strong as any fir tree hung with combs
To drop like bombshells at whoever comes.
My knowledge can hang nets to catch
The flaming sparks that set the thatch
Alight above the floating towers
Trembling to whiteness under bowers
Lit suddenly, and changed to gold,
When the sun awakes and calls his fold.
And when like gleaming jewels they lie
And fill the webs with coloured sky,
I hold some in my hand like fruit,
And point to them and shew their suit
Fiery with splendour and the green
Lawns on which the proud birds preen
Feathers more gorgeous in their glow.
But leagues above the cooling flow
And running rivulets of wind,
Spanning the clouds, one foot behind
Resting upon the giant hills,
Down which the sunlight runs its rills,
The ideal pyramid will raise
Its pinnacle too proud for praise,
And, like a diamond, writes a name,
Across the skies, to give me fame.
And so, while smaller men may make
The soft singing and the golden shake
With which the ripe fields greet the sun,
Into the joys for which they run
Tired lives into a broken mould,
And then renounce the joy and fold
Crippled limbs, rehearsing in their mind,
Sights to remember when quick eyes go blind;
I can reach above the crowd
Without a mask, without a shroud,
And watch them counting grains of sand
To tell the height my buildings stand.

Sensuous, cloud-capped, glittering and dusky, the work
of Sacheverell Sitwell will be remembered, not as a

twentieth-century curiosity in a mad lumber-room, but as the dignified utterance of a poet of extraordinary sensibility. It will be read when the flat, photographic verse of many writers today has long lost what little blood and breath it ever had.

A Greeting
William Walton

'Conduct and work grow coarse and coarse the soul'.

The opposite is the case of Sacheverell Sitwell—'Sachie', the youngest and to my mind the most gifted, and at the same time, neglected of that formidable trio who influenced an entire generation.

I first met him at Oxford in 1920 and to his encouragement and enthusiasm I owe a great deal in those young days of my career. His contribution to English Literature is of considerable significance and is still not fully recognised. He is to me the true lyric poet, sensitive, deeply musical, quite uncompromising toward fashion or facile success. I am convinced that the time will come when he will take his place among our major poets.

> Lean on your balcony! look down!
> My strings shall sing

And so they will, Sachie—dear and constant friend.

Sacheverell Sitwell's Books on Music · *Humphrey Searle*

If I may begin on a personal note, it was Sacheverell Sitwell's *Liszt*, published in 1934, which first aroused my interest in this composer. I was an undergraduate at the time, and had been brought up on a severely classical diet of Bach, Beethoven and Brahms: our teachers told us to despise Liszt as 'flashy and vulgar'. However, a friend of mine showed me the *Années de Pèlerinage*, which certainly does not fit this description, and Sacheverell Sitwell's book, by so vividly evoking not only the character of the man but also the times in which he lived, as well as giving a brilliant account of his contemporaries such as Paganini, Chopin and Berlioz, completed my conversion. In fact I was able to give a Liszt concert at Oxford in 1936 (the 50th anniversary of Liszt's death) which included a number of his late experimental works, unknown at that time, as well as the first English public performance of the *Malediction* for piano and strings, conducted by Constant Lambert, and Sacheverell Sitwell was kind enough to attend and to bring with him that great Liszt pianist Louis Kentner: I am glad to say that I have known both of them ever since.

Sacheverell Sitwell has defined his attitude to writing about music in his Mozart book, published in 1932: he says he has 'tried to convey the atmosphere of Mozart's music, to examine what things may have been in his brain when he wrote it, and to state what effect it produces on sensitive, if untrained, ears'. This seems an admirable statement of his point of view: unlike many professional writers of music, he always keeps the reader's interest aroused, and, apart from his very perceptive comments on the music itself, he relates his chosen composers to their backgrounds and shows how their circumstances affected their works. Thus the Mozart book contains four succinct biographical chapters, a character study of Mozart which gives an interesting account of his family life, a short account of his similarities to or differences from later composers such as Schubert, and several chapters in which most of the major works and some of the minor ones are discussed, all in a lively and unpedantic manner. Sitwell is acute in his account of Mozart's various styles, his earlier rococo writing being altered by his later study of North German music, particularly Bach's, and also in his discussion of the difference between Mozart's and Haydn's symphonies: he remarks, justly: 'Verdi could never have made *The Magic Flute*, with its puerile fancies, into a supreme work of art'. He was perhaps unfair to *Idomeneo*, which in 1932 did not have the standing it has to-day, but his account of *Così Fan Tutte* is excellent, and he quotes Mozart's famous and important letter about the way in which he worked, his method of 'pre-composition'. He refers also to Mozart's physical appearance and state of health—he was small, pale and delicate compared with the robust Haydn—and says of his character: 'he had the gayest and most mercurial nature, encouraged by the slightest turn of fortune, and, as easily, thrown into despair'—here differing from the more pertinacious Beethoven.

His Liszt book, easily the most important biography of him in the English language, was republished in a revised version in 1955 and again in 1966: it is an incomparable account of nineteenth-century musical and social life and also contains an acute character study of its subject and of many other musicians of the period, including even such lesser-known ones as Alkan, Anton Rubinstein and John Field. Sitwell's perceptive appreciation of Liszt's music can be seen, for instance, in his remarks about Liszt's second Ballade, which he contrasts with those of Chopin: 'it is less passionate and more full-blooded:

concerned, as it were, less with personal suffering than
with great happenings on the epical scale, barbarian
invasions, cities in flames—tragedies of public, more than
private, import'. There is no need for me to give any
further quotations. I can only say that this book is
indispensable for anyone who wants to understand not
only Liszt but the whole background of nineteenth-
century musical life. Sacheverell Sitwell also contributed a
short but interesting 'character study' of Liszt to Alan
Walker's symposium, *Franz Liszt, the Man and His Music*
(London 1970).

The other two pre-war books are lighter. *A Background
for Domenico Scarlatti*, published in 1935 for the 250th
anniversary of Scarlatti's birth, gives a vivid account of
the various places where Scarlatti lived—Naples, where he
was born, Venice, where he met the remarkable Irish
composer Thomas Roseingrave, who became a lifelong
admirer of his, Rome, where he was *maestro di cappella* at
St. Peter's, and finally Portugal and Spain, where he
lived for many years. Sitwell discusses the extent of the
influence of Spanish music on Scarlatti's works: it was
said of him that 'he imitated the melody of the tunes sung
by carriers, muleteers and common people', and his
sonatas certainly contain a number of guitar effects. As the
title implies, Sitwell's book discusses the social background
of Scarlatti's time rather than the works in detail, but it
contains many perceptive remarks about the music, and
also gives an interesting account of a Spanish ballet
by another Italian who visited Spain later, Boccher-
ini.

Sitwell's book on Offenbach, published in 1937, is
frankly a divertissement using *La Vie Parisienne* as a thread:
it evokes the atmosphere of Paris in the 1860s, but also
considers the operetta in some detail, as well as discussing
Offenbach in comparison with Rossini on the one hand
and Johann Strauss on the other, and it contains a brilliant
tribute to Offenbach's genius. There are of course many
references to music in Sitwell's other books, and I cannot

think of any other writer and poet who not only has such a real understanding of music but is also able to convey his feelings about it so clearly and brilliantly to his readers.

A Message · *Thornton Wilder*

'I owe to him in particular an intensified appreciation of the Baroque in Southern Italy—of the churches of Bavaria and Austria—and of the late Baroque domestic architecture in Holland. His extraordinary learning and patient research widened our knowledge of such deeply entrenched concepts, in the Middle Ages, as the "Ship of Fools" and the "Dance of Death". We are to be felicitated, but first of all *he* is to be felicitated, on the life-long possession of so rich and learned a play of mind among objects of beauty and rarity.'

The Renaissance
Aptitude · *John Piper*

I first became conscious of the name Sacheverell Sitwell
in 1924, when *Southern Baroque Art* was published. He was
only twenty-seven when that came out, and I thought it
was the most wonderful book—I still think so, indeed. It
showed a completely revolutionary approach to architecture, which seemed to be the reverse of all I'd been taught
by my elders and betters. One now recognises, of course,
that it was not the reverse, but simply a fresh channel of
approach to the whole subject. His descriptions of places
were staggeringly good and impressive, and the whole
book just made a profound impression on me.

The point of the book, in a sense, I suppose, was that it
came from a properly educated—personally educated—
amateur, in the old, proper sense of the word. That's what
I admired so much about it. He has been an untiring
interpreter of art to the ordinary reader, and his range is
quite unexpected, I think; one thought that he would go
on writing books like *Southern Baroque Art* (and in some
ways, I suppose, one was disappointed that he didn't!);
but the range is so wide that one can forgive him anything.
He has, really, in that sense a Renaissance aptitude.

I've never worked with him; indeed I never knew him
for years. I knew Osbert, first, of all the Sitwells—though
I think I must have met Sachie at the time that I got
involved in *Façade* when it was produced at the Aeolian
Hall in 1941, and when I designed the third drop-
curtain used for that work. I remember him as being
above all things sensitive; he was more obviously sensitive
in appearance than his brother or sister, at face value,
though they all have very sensitive features and faces.

Sachie's features looked very searching, but also very vulnerable.

Before the days of *Façade*, I remember being very impressed by a performance of *Rio Grande*, Constant Lambert's setting for chorus, orchestra and piano of Sachie's poem, which first appeared in 1929, but which I had read in his collection of poems, *The Thirteenth Caesar*, which Grant Richards had published in 1924.

After *Southern Baroque Art*, I had curiously enough looked forward to his publications more as an admirer of his poetry than anything else; I was always a reader of his poetry, and tried to read all of it as it came out. I didn't quite so much keep up with all the big visual anthological volumes with commentaries—though I did read, I remember, *Bridge of the Brocade Sash*, about a journey to Japan, a good deal later, in 1959. He is of course a very good topographical writer; I don't think he's written very much about England, except that book which I admired (though Sachie thought I didn't admire)—*British Architects and Craftsmen*, which I reviewed in *The Listener* when it came out in 1945. He was very annoyed with me, and cross, because I made one criticism of the book: I was cross because he failed to see the point of anything after Georgian (or pretended to fail to see the point!). I commented unfavourably on the fact that he expressed himself as seeing nothing in Victorian church architecture; and he was very rebuffed, and I had the rough side of his tongue!

I'm very pleased that he has gone on making his contribution to writing on the arts with the dilettante approach in a German-art-history-dominated age; there's still a great deal to be said for it—and I think really that the so-called 'scholarly' approach of our time has to be tempered with the dilettante approach, or the scholars have it all their own way and become the most frightful—and misleading—bores. An emotional response to these things has to be made before you can react against it, before you can have any constructive view of the thing at all. Just to list things and measure things and size things up as it were physically, doesn't mean anything when the things are visual. You must, I think, allow for a potent emotional reaction; without it you don't strike any fire out of the thing at all.

Sachie is the most splendid companion with whom to experience anything: he has the great quality of not balking at any of the arts, he reads across them all—that's another thing I like about him; he argues from one to the other, which is a frightfully dangerous thing to do, which careful people never dream of doing, but which Sachie does with great verve and splendour and wit, and I think with excellent results, very often.

For instance I have a great admiration for his book on *Liszt* (1934); that was surely the first modern, favourable approach to Liszt, and preceded the great swing back to him which has since happened, with Mr. Searle and Mr. Ogden, and so on; but they all came after Sachie. He's always ignored fashion, and the Lisztian approach to life has always been very sympathetic to him.

In conversation with Derek Parker.

Welcomed as a
Friend · *John Rothenstein*

During the First World War, greatly moved by a poem in *The Nation*,* signed 'Miles', I wrote to its author. Shortly afterwards I received a friendly letter from the Western Front. It was signed 'Osbert Sitwell'. About six years later, probably in the autumn of 1923, I met by chance the author with his brother and sister, and was touched by Osbert's immediate recollection of my schoolboy letter. All three, without preliminaries, welcomed me as a friend.

To be welcomed as a friend is always a pleasure, but such welcome by the Sitwells had a special significance, for one of their many engaging characteristics was their sharp division of the people they knew into friends or enemies; even those whom they did not know were potential friends or potential enemies. Not for them, as for most people, the grey intermediate class of casual acquaintance. If one was a friend, one was implicitly trusted, their house—2 Carlyle Square, Chelsea—always open. (Even now, half a century after my first visit and decades since they left it, I cannot pass it by without a nostalgic pang.)

As a friend one became a participant in their continuous warfare for light against darkness—darkness personified by schoolmasters, telephone-operators who gave wrong numbers (no dialling in those days), Royal Academicians, the sort of person whom at Oxford we used to call 'hearties', but above all those who had shown themselves unfriendly—by hostile reviews and the like—to the Sitwells or their friends.

* *Rhapsode*, published 27 October 1917.

Their own strategy in this warfare was not one of aggression but of 'dynamic defence', and their ripostes were a frequent topic of conversation. One evening, I remember, a well-known hostess telephoned to invite them to some function in a manner which Osbert thought discourteous. 'No, I'm afraid we *can't*,' I heard him say, 'but won't you dine with *us*, *last* Thursday at eight?'

Edith lived in a flat in Bayswater but was constantly at the Carlyle Square house. Here I saw for the first time paintings by Modigliani and Gaudier-Brzeska, and among family portraits also hung works by Picasso, Sickert, and other contemporaries. So numerous were the objects the house contained that its effect was Victorian rather than that of the pioneering centre that it was.

In this volume of tributes to Sachie I have written of the Sitwells as though they were a single entity, which indeed they almost were. It was chance that brought me, for a time, into a relation with Sachie that was particularly close. Among other intimate friends of mine were two beautiful Canadian sisters, Frances and Georgia Doble, with whom, apart from the homes of our parents, we met mostly in frivolous places, nightclubs and the like. Although intelligent and well read, they knew no one in the London literary world. 'You know people who write books,' one of them said to me. 'Couldn't you arrange for us to meet some?' Accordingly I asked Osbert whether I might bring the Doble sisters to see them. 'If you must,' he said.

The day after our visit—there are certain things one remembers, decades later, with trance clearness, as though they happened yesterday; there are others which one (at least I) can forget at once—I saw Osbert in Piccadilly. He was walking west at the Burlington Arcade; I was on the other side walking in the opposite direction, and I crossed the street (then quite a feasible undertaking) and thanked him for his kindness to my friends. 'But we *liked* them,' he said, 'Sachie particularly one.' Thus began a protracted courtship which did not always run smoothly, and as I was so close a friend of both Georgia and Sachie, and, I believe, trusted by both, they used to consult me. One night in August 1924, staying at Weston Hall, Sachie's house in Northamptonshire, I was woken up successively by Osbert, Willie Walton (at that time an honorary member of the family), and finally Sachie himself, in order to discuss some difficulty that had loomed up suddenly. It was evidently resolved, for they were married the following year.

Sachie, tall, lanky, often smiling as though with enjoyment of some joke, was phenomenally well-read. There was little about architecture, painting, and several other subjects, in French, Spanish, Italian, and German, as well as English, that he had not read. This he sometimes spoke of, not boastfully, but mournfully, as someone might say 'I don't know what to do; you see I've read every readable book in the ship's library.' I often heard him question people with a view to finding some obscure book on one of his favoured subjects.

Like Osbert and Edith, he spoke in a drawling voice, choosing his words with great deliberation, as though he had something so informative or amusing to impart—as was usually the case—that it must be imparted with the utmost precision. But unlike some other good talkers, Sachie (again like Osbert and Edith) was always eager to hear what their friends had been doing, where they had been, whom met, what read, and ready to enter into any situation, tragic or comic, in which they happened to be involved.

Soon after we married, Elizabeth and I were their fellow guests at a very large party in Kensington Square. I introduced Sachie to her, and seeing that she, having just come from America, knew scarcely anybody present and was shy, he found her a chair, stood beside her (Harold Acton on the other side) and devoted the greater part of the evening to her entertainment.

I have written about Sachie, though happily flourishing, in the past tense because my two years in the United States and his and Georgia's move to the country broke our habit of meeting constantly, and we have seen each other comparatively rarely of later years. But neither my affection nor my admiration for him have diminished.

A Friend for All
Seasons · *Cyril Beaumont*

It must be almost fifty years ago when first I made the acquaintance of Sacheverell Sitwell, the youngest member of the trio destined to create a stir in the world of art and literature. He was then a young man at Eton, some 15 or 16 years of age.

As I had shown a definite aptitude in the study of inorganic chemistry, it seemed appropriate that my youthful efforts should lead to a possible career as research chemist. But, by one of those inexplicable quirks of fortune, I changed horses in mid-stream and, forsaking science for literature, became a secondhand bookseller in the Charing Cross Road. At this time my knowledge of the arts was conventional, but with the arrival of Pavlova in 1910, followed a little later by Diaghilev's Ballets Russes, I became interested in ballet and in Russian art and literature, which opened up a whole new world to me. I tried to stock such relevant publications as I could find, and it may be that the sight of my shop window displaying reproductions of designs by Bakst, Benois, and Roehrich attracted attention. Soon, I was receiving from a Mr. Sacheverell Sitwell at Eton College orders accompanied by a postal order for this or that souvenir programme, followed by requests for information regarding books on artists quite unknown to me.

It was a red letter day for me when my correspondent called at the shop, affording me an opportunity to make his personal acquaintance. He was a tall, fair, fine looking young man, with handsome clean-shaven features, cast in patrician mould, a little reminiscent of a portrait of a Hanoverian worthy.

I was most impressed by his charming manner and friendliness, and by the wide range of his interests. He had a lively sense of humour coupled with a subtle wit, though less dry and sardonic than that of his brother Osbert. In after years during the First World War, both brothers were in the Grenadier Guards, and thus uniformed they made an impressive couple, clad in their grey greatcoats and peaked caps edged with gold braid, as they strolled down the Charing Cross Road.

Such was the beginning of an acquaintance which ripened into a friendship which has endured for half a century. Perhaps this was due in part to his also being interested in certain subjects which attracted me: the history of ballet; the Romantic Era; the history of the theatre, the *Commedia dell'Arte* in particular; the history of military uniform; and Napoleon III and the Grand Epoque.

But Sachie as he prefers to be addressed by friends, has an extraordinary range of artistic interests: Art, both classical and modern, nor are his studies confined to Europe, he is as much at home among the Japanese painters of the Ukiyô-e School as he is in the realm of Gothic art; Literature, both poetry and prose, classical and modern; Music; Travel; and Food and Drink. From these varied roots have stemmed book after book, describing his impressions and views on the subject under discussion.

Sachie has an unusual way of looking at things. Examining architecture and paintings, he discovers new beauties which had been passed by, or merits which had been overlooked. On the other hand, he keeps abreast with, and even ahead of, the work of rising young painters and new movements.

Sachie was kind enough to write a Preface to my *History of Harlequin*, published in 1926. Among those who reviewed the book was Gordon Craig, then editing *The Mask*, his magazine of the Theatre. He expressed approval of my text and production of the book. But after praising the Preface he observed: 'Mr. Sitwell seems to have nothing to do, so why doesn't he become a publisher and issue these things for the Public'. Continuing in this strain he hinted that Mr. Sitwell should become my patron and support my ventures like a Prince of the Renaissance.

That Sachie should have 'nothing to do' must provoke hilarity, for few writers can be more industrious, or more catholic in their tastes. His output as poet, prose writer, and critic over the years is impressive to a degree, moreover the writing is infused with both style and colour, volume is matched by quality.

Few can rival him in describing a painting, a stately home, a piece of music, or a landscape. He has stimulated new interest in the Baroque. He can write a study of Liszt and his music; extol the genius of Paganini; and yet delight in the gay sparkling melodies of Offenbach, so redolent of the Second Empire. Sachie can evoke the sight, smell, and sound of a North African *souk*, and describe the green tea of Japan, analysing its flavour and substance with something of the concentrated examination devoted by Proust to the taste of his famous 'madeleine'. Sachie is an adept at what he aptly styles 'truffle-hunting': searching for strange, unusual, or fantastic information caught in the rake of his wide reading.

Yet with all his merits and his striking literary achievements one cannot help feeling that he has never received the recognition he so well deserves. To the best of my knowledge no academic laurels have been set upon his brow. Can it be that to admit of the existence of three geniuses in one family is too much to expect? Admittedly his prose is not that of a *popular* writer in the accepted sense of the word, for he is not always easy to read. He is best read slowly and savoured, but how rewarding is the effort! It is difficult, too, to appreciate to the full his subtle allusions; for the reader needs to be as erudite as he is, and that is a standard hard of attainment.

Sachie has been a wonderful friend to me over long years, always interested in my various projects and often supporting them by purchase of some of the products.

For instance, to mention a few examples only, my experiments in book-binding intended to establish an appropriate mood in which to read the contents; my painting of pottery inspired by the examples of those decorated by Wolmark; my founding of the Beaumont Press for the production in finely printed editions of verse and prose by distinguished contemporary authors.

The late Sir Osbert in his *curriculum vitae* in *Who's Who* stated 'educated during the holidays from Eton'. I might say with no less truth that to a considerable extent I have been educated, artistically considered, by Diaghilev's Ballets Russes and the Sitwell brothers.

So far as my personal knowledge is concerned, Sachie has only one phobia, a dread of catching the common cold. If the person with whom he is conversing suddenly reveals a slight thickness of speech, or indulges in a repeated blowing of the nose, or, worst of all, a sneeze, Sachie abruptly vanishes as though at the touch of a magician's wand.

The Pursuit of
Excellence · *Christian Hesketh*

When I first met Sachie I was very young, and it therefore surprised me when what I found in him was not
entirely what I expected. He was very distinguished: but
this, of course, was no more than I had already been told.
One of his books, and a great classic it is, *Southern Baroque
Art*, was known to me before we met, so, unfamiliar to
him as I then was, he still found in me one of his many
readers.

Even so stimulating an introduction gave me no hint,
however, of the treat awaiting me, and for which, as it
turned out, I was wholly unprepared. We met, and though
the occasion was in no way remarkable, it is still one
that in all its details lingers on in my mind. The qualities
that were his then, belong to him still. Even so, what
astonished me in the beginning was to find that what I
saw through his eyes added both warmth and irony to all
that I observed, so much of which, in any case, I would not
have noticed but in his company.

Twenty years later, it is still my rare privilege to live
in the same part of England as he, and for the first time in
my life, some months ago, I was asked to introduce him
as the speaker at our County Art Gallery, where an exhibition in honour of Venice was at that time about to open.
Inspired by this occasion, quite suddenly, I found myself
putting into words the thoughts, the sentiments, that for
so long, to my shame, I had kept to myself. On this one
occasion I was happy and even inspired to speak, feeling,
as I did, that the debt I owed was not only one I shared
with everyone in my audience, but came into a category
that we are all too prone to ignore until inevitably the

73

day dawns when we long, and it is too late, to put into words what hitherto we have done no more than feel. So for these reasons, and others too, I welcomed even so modest an opportunity as the one chance had afforded me, to speak of Sachie; and when I had finished, it was a delight to discover that most of those present had come to the exhibition above all for Sachie's sake, to hear, applaud, and speak to one whose entire life has been spent in the pursuit of excellence, yet still has something to offer even the humblest of admirers. And that something is quite hard to define, because in him we have a bird of paradise whose shadow has fallen on so many different scenes that it comes as no surprise to discover that even in far Peru, the freedom of the city of Lima has been conferred on him.

Often, in all too many of his activities, I saw very little of him, but once, travelling by car through Yorkshire with him and his wife, I did see the bird of paradise in flight, and this was for me so idyllic an experience that when addressing the crowds at the art gallery I felt unwilling to share with them a memory so private and so magical. Sachie and Georgia wished to look at certain sights in Yorkshire, and happy to be included in such an expedition I set off with them. From the beginning, it was Sachie who decided where we were to go, and like some inspired truffle-hound, he was seldom if ever at fault. As his energy was no less resourceful, I began to feel each evening that like a dazzled child I was taking part in some form of treasure hunt which, day by day, was getting more exciting.

Like all perfectionists, he could not bear to do anything in a slapdash way, and on one memorable occasion he induced an increasingly irate Georgia to stop the car in more than one awkward place on a perpendicular hill road, so that we should see and admire Richmond from the best possible viewpoint. The last time this happened the brake was applied with something more than a snap, and as Sachie alighted he said one word, very reproach-fully, to the still seething driver: 'Crosspatch.' Need I say that for the rest of the trip his wishes came first?—and as our journey proceeded, I marvelled at the way in which by instinct, as well as through knowledge, he singled out for attention (and this happened wherever we went) only what was most worth seeing.

In doing so, all his qualities, or, as they seemed in his case, the bird of paradise's feathers, were so brightly visible that never afterwards could I think of them as merely human attributes, or as anything less than dazzling to a beholder. Every day was too short for what we hoped to do; but even so, there was still time for surprise. On the very last morning, we visited a small remote village, and here Sachie found, to his joy, the very same confectionery where in his childhood he had often bought sweets. It was quite unlike anything else I have ever seen, and so old that beside it we all seemed like children.

Ever since, I have wondered where it was, and if indeed I ever saw it—because I do remember, during that one week, seeing more than I ever have since. Only the other day I was reminded of this, when reading one of the poems from his latest book, *Tropicalia*. In it, he refers to lands 'Where the day-long dresses could be made of flowers.' And as I thought of these words, I remembered that once, in his company, I had seen such sights, and even felt that I, too, was wearing just such a garment.

A Guardee for
Dinner · *Diana Cooper*

'What is a guardee?' I asked one day aged 18. Emerald
Cunard answered, 'You shall have one at dinner tonight.'
Now I knew it was a sort of soldier but of what kind or
rank I was ignorant, so she sketched me a picture of high
military discipline, of high social standing, and of high
conventionalism. Imagine then my surprise when the first
words of my guardee, Osbert Sitwell, were, 'What do you
really think of Stravinsky?'

Now my upbringing had taught me a little about composers, Russians, operas, ballets,—and nothing whatever
about echelons, so I suppose I held a view about Stravinsky, and our conversation sped along merrily enough
and continued to do so on and off for most of our lives.

In the first war I lay for months in a London nursing
home with a fractured leg—a cheerful room full of flowers
and young people and pinioned birds on fruit trees, and
20 gas balloons floating at various levels between ceiling
and floor, and to this nonsense bedside Osbert one day
brought his kid brother Sachie—a tall innocent boy in
uniform—looking to my older pitying eyes too tender and
frail and quite unfit for the fearful trenches of Flanders.

So now I knew two guardees, and never since have I met
one that compares in any way with the Sitwell brothers.
Their famous sister, Edith, alas, I never saw, but Osbert
till his death, Sachie with his loved and loving wife,
Georgia, have spent many happy, happy times together—
in other countries and in their enchanting house, Weston.
I love to think of them there. Pray that till my sands run
out they will love me, and spoil me and make me laugh
as they always have.

A Mutual
Scarborough · *Susan Hill*

In the month of thunder, in the noise of timber,
I was born in November by the stormy sea.

from Upon an Image by Dante *by Sacheverell Sitwell*

Sacheverell Sitwell was born in The Crescent, Scarborough, in November 1897. I was born half a mile from there and by the same 'stormy sea' in February 1942.

The town of Scarborough, and the coastline and countryside belonging to it, had changed little in those forty-four years intervening between our births. Indeed, it has changed remarkably little now. I no longer live there, but often visit, and quite regularly dream about it. So does Sachie.

I think it is a beautiful town. It is set on the top of high cliffs, out of which gardens have been carved here and there—the Italian Garden, the Rose Garden for the Blind —and down between the trees, growing out of those cliffs, primroses and aconites sprout in the very early, very cold spring.

Many of the buildings, particularly on the older, south side of the town, are Regency and Victorian, in curving crescents like those of Nash; others, like the Sitwell house, Wood End, and the home of Sacheverell's grandparents, Londesborough Lodge, are imposing villas.

Scarborough is, of course, a thriving seaside resort—it always was: the Victorians discovered it and came in droves to drink the restorative (and revolting) spa waters. In the summer, Scarborough fills up with charabancs and caravans, the beaches are packed, there are ice-cream and bingo and winkle stalls—but all confined to the lower foreshore and the North Bay end of the town. The South Bay, that half in which Sachie and I were born, has always been quieter, more residential, and much favoured by the rich and the retired. (In fact, the South Bay is rather snobbish and likes to keep itself aloof from the North Bay and what were always known in my childhood as 'the trippers'.)

But in the winter everything changes and it is the winters there of which Sachie and I have remarkably similar recollections. There are no 'trippers' then—only north-east winds cutting you in half, and scudding grey skies, and enormous seas with waves a hundred feet high roaring over the rocks and rearing up high into the air, to crash, white and seething, on to the foreshore road, and the Marine Drive. There is very often snow from December until the end of March. There are almost always one or two dramatic lifeboat rescues.

I cannot remember when I first learned about the Sitwell family, but there never seems to have been a time when I did not know of, and think about, them, so I must have been very young. It was probably the first year I suffered from a beastly winter disease called 'croup' (Sachie had it, too, and his memories of it are identical to mine). Croup often follows (as in my case) whooping-cough, and it recurs winter after winter. I had it badly every year until I was nine or ten. There is a terrible cough, and a sore chest, and one of the remedies (which never, I think, actually worked) was a nauseating concoction called Ipecacuanha wine. Osbert Sitwell mentions it in the first volume of his autobiography, *Left Hand, Right Hand*. He calls it 'that searing drug which even its name, with, in its mournful but fascinating rhythms, all the lilting tangos of South America, can never redeem'.

Thankfully, other and much more effective, treatment was prescribed for me. (Sachie had to put up with Ipecacuanha.) I was taken, every day for a month, to have Sun-Ray (ultra-violet) treatment and this was administered at Londesborough Lodge—since the war, a medical centre.

I was told at once that this very handsome house used to belong to the grandparents of 'the famous Sitwells'. I asked who these Sitwells were and was told their names and that they were 'very famous poets and writers'. I heard that their mother had been a great beauty and their father an eccentric baronet. (I had no idea what 'eccentric baronet' could possibly mean.) They were all spoken of in a tone of awed affection. Scarborough still thought of the family as belonging to itself.

It was their names I thought so impressive and when I was first taken to their house, Wood End, I stood trans-fixed in front of the Sargent portrait reciting 'Osbert, Edith and Sacheverell' under my breath. But it was 'Sacheverell' which most appealed to me. I thought it a most beautiful name. (I still do.) I called one of my dolls 'Sacheverell' at once.

The Crescent meant to me both Sun-Ray treatment, and 'Sunday afternoons'. These were very special. We walked down the Valley Road and climbed up the steep paths until we came out just below the gardens of Wood End. (In the elm trees high above us, rooks nested, and one of my earliest memories is the sound of their cawing—Sachie tells me that it was one of his ancestors who brought rooks to Scarborough, from somewhere abroad.)

When Londesborough Lodge became a medical centre, Wood End became a natural history museum. On those Sunday afternoons, we first went in to look at rooms full of stuffed seagulls and foxes, and of lumps of jet and cornelian, found in plenty in the neighbouring bays, at Whitby and Cornelian. Then we went into the conserva-tory. This was my favourite place and to those hours I spent in it, I owe a lifelong passion for all Victorian conservatories and their plants. It is the smell of them which is always evocative—the conservatory at Weston reminds me at once, if I close my eyes and sniff, of Wood End. The conservatory there was built by Sir George Sitwell, and he stocked it, not only with exotic plants and trees, but with exotic birds too. Those are now safely caged (or rather, their ancestors are). But Osbert Sitwell has written about how they flew about and often flew into the ballroom over the heads of the evening's guests.

The only way I could be coaxed out of the conservatory was by a promise of a visit, up a tiny, twisting staircase, to 'the Sitwell Rooms'. In there are portraits of the three artists, together with a large number of manuscripts and notebooks, first editions and other relicts, displayed in glass cases. I studied them, entranced, at the age of five or six, and I knew bits of *Façade* and the first half of Sachie's poem *Rio Grande* by heart, simply because some books were open at those pages. The three Sitwells played a tremendous part in my imagination, but it was Sacheverell of whom I thought most—the one with the magic name, and the one who, perhaps because he was the youngest, felt somehow nearer to me.

We left Scarborough when I was fifteen. By then, I knew an enormous amount about the Sitwell past, from Osbert Sitwell's autobiography, and the poems of all three. But I had also discovered a great deal about the rest of the wide world, and its oddities and beauties, from Sachie's books. I suppose that he must have seen more beautiful and amazing places and people and works of art in his lifetime than anyone else at all. Certainly, I am continually amazed by what he knows. I was re-reading a collection of his newspaper articles, *Truffle Hunt*, recently, and there seems to be a fascinating and informative article on everything under the sun. Having a conversation with Sachie is rather like dipping into a treasure trove—you simply never know what will come up, but it's always something marvellous.

Because, to my astonishment, I met him at last, this legendary Sacheverell, so much a part of my own childhood. I had been thinking, a year or so ago, about Scarborough and the Sitwells, and had the idea of doing a radio programme, in which I would talk at length to Sachie. In slight trepidation, I wrote about it to him, and had (of course) a charming reply, in which he told me, 'I am decidedly interested in Scarborough and cannot help it and always will be,' and invited me to luncheon.

I discovered that Weston was only forty minutes' drive from where I live, in Leamington Spa, I borrowed a B.B.C. tape recorder, and I went. I was extremely nervous. I could scarcely believe, when we shook hands, that I was here and Sachie was there, in the flesh, the one I had liked best in the family portrait, the one with the beautiful name.

That first visit of mine to Weston Hall was a delight and a disaster. I was made to feel at home, and we had a delicious and friendly luncheon. But when I came to try and record some of our conversation, disaster struck. The tape recorder was faulty, and I am very bad at anything electrical and/or mechanical. I fiddled and fiddled with the wretched thing, and Sachie was very patient, and it would *not* work. I spent the best part of an hour trying to get it to go, which, after a fashion, it eventually did. By then, I only wanted the ground to open up and swallow me.

In the event, the proposed radio programme came to nothing. Never mind. As Georgia Sitwell said, 'At least it brought us together.' Which it did, and now I go often, though never often enough, to Weston, that fine, honey-coloured house, and Sachie and Georgia are dear, generous friends. And almost always, Sachie and I have something to say to each other about Scarborough, that haunting town of our childhoods 'by the stormy sea'.

Looking and
Learning · *Geoffrey Elborn*

When considering any of them, it is a mistake to think of 'the Sitwells'. As Edith Sitwell herself remarked, 'we do not like to be treated as if we were an aggregate Indian God, with three sets of legs and arms, but otherwise indivisible. We are individual artists, and the fact that we are brothers and sisters is the business of nobody else considering our work.'

For in spite of an early family likeness in work, perhaps due to their influence on each other, working in the beautiful but tragic Renishaw, their work from 1920 onwards showed that they were distinct writers, with something distinct to say.

Osbert Sitwell was noted in the 1920s as a satirist, having published *The Winstonburg Line, Enoch Arden* and *Miss Mew.* He was then sharing a house with his brother in Carlyle Square, where William Walton also lived for a time; with Edith Sitwell, they all prepared *Façade* there in 1922. Sacheverell had published his first book of poems, *The People's Palace,* in 1918. Of him, T. S. Eliot wrote (when some of the poems first appeared in *Wheels*):

The most important and most difficult poet in the volume. In fact the best that has appeared for several years. He has an idiom which looks at first sight like rhetoric, and one finds with a shock that the words have values. He tends in his weaker moments to go off like a beautiful but ineffectual aeroplane, beating its propellors vainly against a tree, but when he has a definite concrete sensation as in *The Feathered Hat,* he is all right.

In his first prose book, *Southern Baroque Art,* he showed a fascination with and clear understanding of art. Not just any passing, fashionable art, but art which had hitherto been neglected, and through that book he revived a new interest in baroque art in Italy and elsewhere.

Edith had in 1914 escaped the difficulties of her parents' environment, and come to live in Moscow Road, London, with her governess, Helen Rootham (the translator of Rimbaud's *Les Illuminations*). After the publication of the first volume of her magazine *Wheels*, in 1916, she was visited by such diverse figures as W. B. Yeats, T. S. Eliot and Cecil Beaton. It was also during her stay in Moscow Road that she published her first collection of poems, *The Mother* (1915).

So Edith wrote poetry, Osbert was a noted satirist; but when it comes to pinning down Sacheverell, it is like trying to hold down the delicate wings of a beautiful moth, only to find that there are many more, fluttering in all directions. For Sacheverell felt that his poetry should arise out of inspiration created by an absorption in the arts; he found it necessary to be involved in music, the ballet, painting—really, all manifestations of the created arts. In fact, through this belief his poetry became the means of an extension of his interest *in* the arts.

But this interest was not expressed entirely in poetry. Before Sacheverell published *Canons of Giant Art* in 1933, a collection of poems including *Agamemnon's Tomb*, he had already written a ballet of an English nature for Diaghilev: called *The Triumph of Neptune*, and with music by Lord Berners, it was the most popular ballet of the 1929 London season (choreographed by Balanchine, and danced by Danilova and Lifar, it was based on themes from traditional English pantomime, and set in a *décor* inspired by Pollock's toy theatres).

The contemporary baroque composer with Handel and Bach, Domenico Scarlatti (all three were born in 1685) was the subject of a book—the first definitive study of the composer—which Sacheverell wrote as a 250th birthday present. The study inspired Dr. Ralph Kirkpatrick's full-length biography. (Little had been known of Scarlatti and his background; the enterprising Kirkpatrick, anxious to trace his descendants, did so by looking up the name in a telephone directory.)

Sacheverell's study of Liszt—a full-length biography—is his best study in the musical field, and indeed is constantly being cited as the best book available on its subject. Perhaps there are some aspects of Liszt, that creator of war-horses and fireworks, with which we may also identify Sacheverell; both have a love of the romantic, both show in their work great diversity of content; Liszt was proud of his dress, and Sacheverell has been said to dress like an elegant dandy.

It is in his wonderful, indeed unique fantasies that Sacheverell is at his most personal, giving not only opinions of Picasso or Stravinsky, for example, but statements about himself that are exciting because he has not yet written an autobiography (apart from the autobiographical-fantasy *All Summer in a Day*, which appeared in 1926).

A great deal about the author is to be learned in *Splendours and Miseries* and its companion volume *Journey to the Ends of Time*, his most impressive fantasy. Here he hints of themes still to be explored, and enlarges on what he has already set down on paper, quite apart from numerous new subjects. Of his devotion to Bach, he has written often, and his own work resembles a great fugue. He explores a melodic theme, develops and elaborates it so that we finish with a great gathering of ideas all woven into a final conclusion. This method of presenting a theme is the difficulty but also the pleasure of Sacheverell's work. If one is not prepared to watch and hold all the threads of the tapestry of sounds and words, a lost thread may mean the loss of the work as a whole, and render it meaningless.

Of the diversity of material he has published, Sacheverell has remarked:

The work of the humming bird is the nectar of the flowers. I am aware that some may be reminded of that by my excursions and changes of subject, if any read me in another age, and it is for this reason that I choose the moth as being the more serious and diligent, and the creature, too, of night as well as day. For my chosen topics have not all been pleasant and sunlit any more than the world of my youth, which flowered between two wars. But I have lived to see what I was born to see. I cannot go down in unhappiness after that. It is not *une pauvre terre*, a poor earth, after all. It has splendours as well as miseries to recommend it.

He also notes that by these excursions and changes of subject

There is the torment of having done or tried too many things at once; to which the rejoinder is 'mind your own business'. Music reviewers will not give you a notice because you are not a musician; botanists, ornithologists, ignore you because you are not of them; writers on architecture and kindred subjects chase away the intruder; and by now it is too late to begin another career, and you are forgotten as a poet. But whose fault is that, and who gets the blame? It is better to keep to the straight furrow, looking not to left or right, nor following the hare that runs out of the spinney.

In these excursions, Sacheverell constructs thread on thread, using all his senses, in order to recreate experience exactly. When one reads him, one is aware that his work *is* the object, or place, *there* and *here* in front of one; so much so that it almost becomes a reality. This facility of giving a heightened sense of physical objects is rather like the power of Virginia Woolf. One has only to read Sacheverell Sitwell's *Death of a Fly* and Virginia Woolf's *Death of a Moth* to realise that their work, while very different in approach, combines the same sensitivity, and sense of reality.

But what are these vast tapestries? On what does Sacheverell Sitwell construct his books?

Because of the extent of his work, one cannot detail everything within the limitations of an essay: he has written, as I have said, of music, works of art, places— *Truffle Hunt* is an excellent introduction to his work, and, in tiny essays of sometimes twenty lines, shows his vast range far better than anything else.

A browse through a few of his books (those I have

mentioned, among the fantasies; *Canons of Giant Art*, in poetry; more recently, a poem written after seeing his sister in death) shows his concern with death. Especially in *Splendours and Miseries* and *Journey to the Ends of Time*, and *Agamemnon's Tomb*, he gives a detailed study of his thoughts and conclusions.

He says: 'I do not believe in an after-life . . . the body dies completely, but something is gone at the moment of death—not the soul, but what?' *Journey to the Ends of Time* (in which he wrote that line) is a vast meditation, as the author puts it, on 'the problems and mysteries of life and death, to present the skeleton, to give the bare bones, but not the flesh'. He gives an account of a journey after death through a purgatory and hell, using images drawn from painting and life, all combined with a wonderful and unique visionary sense. He is often gentle, but also deliberately horrifies, always showing compassion. In his autobiographical fantasy, *All Summer in a Day*, he shows concern for the miner's children at Eckington, near his home at Renishaw, just as he is angered by the ill-treatment of children at Tedworth Mill in the nineteenth century, described in *Journey to the Ends of Time*.

There is no declaration of faith in that book, despite the subject matter; and as early as *Splendours and Miseries*, published during the Second World War, Sacheverell stated:

In the case of Bach . . . the true secret is his Christianity. It is upon that assurance that his rolling phrases mount into the heavens. Such are the truths that the Fugues set out to prove. And there is more wisdom in him than in religion; more of truth and beauty than in all the prayers and aspirations. Many faiths; but only the one true Ancient, of whom we hear the huge fist when the formal language of the Fugue begins.

Sacheverell's own lack of faith is confirmed in the preface to *Journey to the Ends of Time*:

One of my deficiencies is that I am not at all religious, and if the truth be known, Christian neither by instinct nor inclination . . . I have listened and heard nothing, although that is no proof, except perhaps in the pealing of an organ or looking to the evening sky through the rose-windows of Chartres.

I remarked earlier that these fantasies show Sacheverell Sitwell at his most personal. In *Journey to the Ends of Time*, he writes of his reputation as a poet, and his hopes for his own poetry; his regret at not having been able to have written it all his life:

To be once more a poet, and not driven to write prose. Poetry that comes to one when young, and one hopes, once more when old, but not yet, though I think I may feel it coming. . . . As one grows older oneself one is the more drawn to those who have not been successful in their lives.

Since writing that in 1959, Sacheverell has written and published his first poetry for over thirty-five years, and more is expected. His poetry is perhaps not better-known, partly because of his long silence as a poet, but also because of the mad and ridiculous 'poetry' that is fashionable, and which unlike the poetry that he writes is shapeless, meaningless and without technique.

It is also true that like his sister, he may have written too much poetry: too much for the casual reader who might be daunted by the size of his collected poems. But there is much to delight, and he may be proud that his admirers have included Roy Campbell, Arthur Waley, Dylan Thomas, and Yeats. If a fault is to be found with his poetry it is that he has written on too similar themes: the poetry tumbles out like a wild but glittering confetti— each poem has quality, but taken as a whole, a poem may sometimes fail.

In attempting to write of the work of Sacheverell Sitwell, I have been constantly aware that I may have been presenting him as a remote, cold aesthete. He is not so. Although he knows more than anyone alive about aspects of art, he does not parade his great knowledge in a way that is condescending. When I met him once in the ethnographical section of the British Museum, near the Royal Academy, he was the perfect guide, expanding on the dull and inadequate labels that were there already. But this was not done in a way that suggested you knew nothing about the exhibit, although that was the truth.

Instead of saying '*This* is a Javanese shadow puppet', for example, he would say, 'This is a Javanese shadow puppet, don't you think?'

And when I nearly led him and a friend down the fire-escape as we were trying to leave, he corrected me in a delightful, tactful way, so that I scarcely noticed my *faux pas*.

In conversation, he always assumes that one knows as much about any subject as he does. When one wants to know more, he will elaborate, often with great humour, sometimes telling a story against himself, and pausing only to smoke a cigarette with great rapidity. As for instance when he told me he was feeling nervous about going to have an exploratory X-ray for a suspected lung disease. This was to involve swallowing a small camera, and he delayed going into the place where it was to be carried out, pacing up and down, feeling more and more nervous. But his fear disappeared, and he hurried in, after observing a small crowd which had gathered round a man who was swallowing swords!

Or the occasion when he and his wife had their luggage sent on, when on holiday abroad, with just enough left on their last day to go exploring caves. The night before the projected visit, Sacheverell left his shoes outside his hotel bedroom door, to be cleaned. In the morning, however, they had disappeared. Enquiries showed that they had been taken away to be repaired; and as that was the only pair of shoes he had, he was marooned in the hotel in his slippers.

His conversation will run from the strange mystery of Glamis Castle, to swans ('I do like the young swans in their little woolly Jaegar suits!') to Pavel Tchelichew. ('He was an energetic person—in thought, at least—and always willing to paint the town red. But his output was greatly diminished, because he spent much of his time worrying that people were plotting and conspiring against him.')

And when the conversation changed to the Madeline Smith affair, of which he had written a reconstruction in *Splendours and Miseries*, he left the room for a moment, and returned with one of the actual love letters written by her.

His tastes in literature include a devotion to the Russian masters, and on a recent *Desert Island Discs* programme, he wanted to take away a copy of *Anna Karenina* and *War and Peace* bound together. In poetry he has a great respect for Dylan Thomas, whom he knew. Like his sister, he praises Swinburne highly, naming *August* and *Anactoria* among his favourites.

As hosts, he and his wife are among the best I know. Sacheverell sticks to a strict writing plan, and when he is working one is free to browse through his large library, listen to his gramophone records, or take walks through his garden. From time to time he will come down to where one is, hoping that one is not bored. That is not possible, for there is everything at Weston Hall to hold the attention of anyone who enjoys art: one may look at his Tiepolo (once his brother's), the collection of work by Severini, or the paintings by the strange Victorian artist Richard Dadd, who in madness killed his father.

One of the most remarkable works in his collection is a Brueghel, which hangs in his study—a smaller version of the famous original which hangs in the Prado, *The Triumph of Death*.

In contemporary art, Picasso is his hero, and he has written of his disappointment at the failure to achieve his ambition to get Picasso to fresco some of the walls of Montegufoni—a failure which arose from a difference between the artist and Sir George Sitwell about the former's fee. Sacheverell knew Modigliani (to whom he was introduced by their mutual friend, Epstein), and was associated with his brother in the presentation of the first post-Impressionist exhibition in London after the First World War.

But it is impossible to mention all the aspects of the

work of Sacheverell Sitwell, who has written over seventy books and edited seventy more, who has dealt with porcelain figures, the Goldberg Variations, Beckford, towers, the *vie Parisienne*, poltergeists, flower books. . . . One can only hope that more people will be encouraged to read his work; and now that his poetry is again appearing, we have proof that in this tawdry age, poetry is still being written.

I should like to thank him publicly for the dedication of a poem to me, and for the debt I owe him—for the worlds he has enabled me to explore through his books, and by the friendship of himself and Lady Sitwell.

I am one of those who would like paradise to be a place to work in. I do not want to rest. Most of all, I want to write poetry. To have the fame of a poet, and a public of a handful of persons. And to look around and learn.

The Goal of all the Arts · *Hugh MacDiarmid*

A tribute to Sacheverell Sitwell
in admiration and gratitude

Where the Paneubiotic Synthesis is grasped in its totality,
Omnilateral aristology obligatory on everybody,
Each having five hundred ethnohistorians within reach,
A thousand philosophies, and being well-acquainted
With the universal masterpieces of literature and the
    fine arts,
And enjoying the perfect vitality that only comes
Through mastering the synthesis and duly welcoming
All the higher thought-currents of love!

This is what our lives have been given to find,
A language that can serve our purposes.
A marvellous lucidity, a quality of fiery aery light,
Flowing like clear water, flying like a bird,
Burning like a sunlit landscape,
Conveying with a positively Godlike assurance,
Swiftly, shiningly, exactly, what we want to convey.
This use of words, this peculiar aptness and handiness,
Adapts itself to our every mood, now pathetic, now ironic,
Now full of love, of indignation, of sensuality, of glamour,
    of glory,
With an inevitable richness of remembered detail
And a richness of imagery that is never cloying,
A curious and indescribable quality
Of sensual sensitiveness,

Of very light and very air itself
—Pliant as a young hazel wand,
Certain as a gull's wings,
Lucid as a mountain stream,
Expressive as the eyes of a woman in the presence of love,
Expressing the complex vision of everything in one,
Suffering all impressions, all experience, all doctrines
To pass through and taking what seems valuable from
    each,
No matter in however many directions
These essences seem to lead.

Civilised being is bound up with values
Unaffected by the destruction of *ce qui ferme*
Because the only *résistance au temps*
Relevant to them is a resistance
Having nothing to do with survival in time.
The objects of an endeavour acceptable
In the light of these values are alone
Invulnerable to the decay of time
Or the disappointment of imperfection;
By their means alone may we approach
The ideal of self-possession and self-coincidence
And become "changed into ourselves by eternity".

Responsibility for the present state of the world
And for its development for better or worse
Lies with every single individual;
Freedom is only really possible
In proportion as all are free.
Knowledge and, indeed, adoption *(Aneignung)*
Of the rich Western tradition
And all the wisdom of the East as well
Is the indispensable condition for any progress;
World-history and world-philosophy
Are only now beginning to dawn;

Whatever tribulation may yet be in store for men
Pessimism is false. Let us make ourselves at home
In das Umgreifende, that super-objective,
The final reality to which human life can attain.
Short of that every man is guilty,
Living only the immediate life,
Without memory, without plan, without mastery.
The very definition of vulgarity;
Guilty of a dereliction of duty,
The 'distraction' of Pascal,
The 'aesthetic stage' of Kierkegaard,
The 'inauthentic life' of Heidegger,
The 'alienation' of Marx,
The self-deception (mauvais foi) of Sartre.

I believe it will be in every connection soon
As already in the field of colour
Where the imitative stage
Has long been passed
And coal tar dyes are synthesised no more
To imitate the colours of nature
Whether of autumn or spring.
The pattern cards of dye-stuff firms to-day
Display multitudes of syntheses
That transcend Nature to teach
Almost a philosophic satisfaction
Of the aesthetic sense of colour.

Apart from a handful of scientists and poets
Hardly anybody is aware of it yet
(A society of people without a voice for the consciousness
That is slowly growing within them)
Nevertheless everywhere among the great masses of
    mankind
With every hour it is growing and emerging
Like a mango tree under a cloth

Stirring the dull cloth
Sending out tentacles.
—It is not something that can be stopped
By sticking it away in a zinc-lined box
Like a tube of radium,
As most people hope,
Calling all who approve of it mad,
The term they always apply
To anyone who tries to make them think.

For Schoenberg was right. The problem involved
In mental realisation
Is not that the evolution of music
Must wait on the human ear,
But that the human ear must catch up
With the evolution of music.
As with Schoenberg's so with your work
And scant though the evidence be
Of progress here we have ample proof
(While yet the vast majority of mankind
Are but inclining to close the infinite gap
And may succeed in a few billion years perhaps)
That the complicated is Nature's climax of rightness
And the simple at a discount.